KAREN BROWN'S
England
Charming Bed &

Written by

JUNE BROWN

Illustrations by Barbara Tapp

Cover Painting by Jann Pollard

Travel Press
Karen Brown's Country Inn Series

Editors: Clare Brown, June Brown, Karen Brown, Iris Sandilands
Technical support: William H. Brown III; Aide-de-camp: William H. Brown
Illustrations: Barbara Tapp; Cover painting: Jann Pollard; Cover design: Tara Brassil
Maps: Susanne Lau Alloway—Greenleaf Design & Graphics: Cover photograph: Elaine Eisenberg
Written in cooperation with Carlson Wagonlit/Town & Country Hillsdale Travel, San Mateo, CA 94401
Copyright © 1988, 1993, 1995, 1996 by Karen Brown's Guides. All rights reserved
This book or parts thereof may not be reproduced in any form without obtaining written
permission from the publisher: Travel Press, P.O. Box 70, San Mateo, CA 94401, tel: (415) 342-9117
Distributed USA & Canada: The Globe Pequot Press
Box 833, Old Saybrook, CT 06475, tel: (860) 395-0440, fax: (860) 395-0312
Distributed Australia & New Zealand: Little Hills Press Pty. Ltd. tel: (02) 437-6995, fax: (02) 438-5762
1st Floor, Regent House, 37-43 Alexander St, Crows Nest NSW 2065, Australia
Distributed Europe: Springfield Books Ltd., tel: (01484) 864 955, fax: (01484) 865 443
Norman Road, Denby Dale, Huddersfield HD8 8TH, W. Yorkshire, England
A catalog record for this book is available from the British Library

Library of Congress Cataloging-in-Publication Data

Brown, June , 1949 -
    Karen Brown's England : charming bed & breakfasts / written by
June Brown ; sketches by Barbara Tapp ; cover painting by Jann
Pollard.
        p. cm.-- (Karen Brown's country inn series)
    Revision of : Karen Brown's English country bed & breakfasts.
    Includes index.
    ISBN 0-930328-38-8 (pbk.)
    1. Bed and breakfast accommodations--England--Guidebooks.
2. England--Guidebooks. I. Brown, June, 1949-   Karen Brown's
English country bed & breakfasts. Karen. II. Title. III. Series.
TX907.3.G72E5436 1996
647.9442'03--dc20   95-42054
                                   CIP

KAREN BROWN'S

England

Charming Bed & Breakfasts

Karen Brown Titles

Austria: Charming Inns & Itineraries

California: Charming Inns & Itineraries

England: Charming Bed & Breakfasts

England, Wales & Scotland: Charming Hotels & Itineraries

French Country Bed & Breakfasts

France: Charming Inns & Itineraries

Germany: Charming Inns & Itineraries

Ireland: Charming Inns & Itineraries

Italy: Charming Bed & Breakfasts

Italy: Charming Inns & Itineraries

Spain: Charming Inns & Itineraries

Swiss Country Inns & Itineraries

Dedicated with All My Love
to My Parents
Gladys and George

Contents

Introduction

Rye

England: Charming Bed & Breakfasts describes special accommodations in tranquil countryside locations, picturesque villages, historic towns, and a selection of cultural cities beyond London. Interspersed with thatched cottages and grand ancestral manors are traditional pubs and guesthouses—all offering wholehearted hospitality in charming surroundings. Every place to stay is one that we have seen and enjoyed—our personal recommendation. We sincerely believe that where you lay your head each night makes the difference between a good and a great vacation. If you prefer to travel the hotel route, or are looking for itinerary suggestions, we trust you'll find just what you need in our companion guide, *England, Wales & Scotland: Charming Hotels & Itineraries*.

About Bed and Breakfast Travel

Every place to stay in this book has a different approach to bed and breakfast. Some households are very informal, some welcome children, and others invite you to sample gracious living, cocktails in the drawing room, billiards after dinner, and croquet on the lawn. The one thing that they have in common is a warmth of welcome. We have tried to be candid and honest in our appraisals and tried to convey each listing's special flavor so that you know what to expect and will not be disappointed. **None of the places to stay ever pays to be included.** To help you appreciate and understand what to expect when staying at places in this guide, the following pointers are given in alphabetical order, not order of importance.

ANIMALS

Even if animals are not mentioned in the write-up, the chances are that there are friendly, tail-wagging dogs and sleek cats as visible members of the families.

ARRIVAL AND DEPARTURE

Always discuss your time of arrival—hosts usually expect you to arrive around 6 pm. If you are going to arrive late or early, be certain to telephone your host. You are expected to leave by 10 am on the morning of your departure. By and large you are not expected to be on the premises during the day.

BATHROOMS

In the listing we state how many rooms have en-suite bathrooms in the bedrooms. Several listings have private bathrooms which means that your facilities are located down the hall.

BEDROOMS

Beds are often made with duvets (down comforters) instead of the more traditional blankets and sheets. A double room has one double bed, a twin room has two single beds, and a family room contains one or more single beds in addition to a double bed. Zip and link beds are very popular: these are twin beds that can be zipped together (linked) to form an American queen-sized bed. American king and queen beds are still few and far between.

CHILDREN

Places that welcome children state "Children welcome." The majority of listings in this guide do not "welcome" children but find they become tolerable at different ages over 5 or, more often than not, over 12. In some cases places simply do not accept children and the listing states "Children not accepted." However, these indications of children's acceptability are not cast in stone, so if you have your heart set on staying at a listing that accepts children over 12 and you have an 8-year-old, call them, explain your situation, and they may well take you. Ideally we would like to see all listings welcoming children and all parents remembering that they are staying in a home and doing their bit by making sure that children do not run wild. A list of places that "welcome" children of any age is given at the back of this book.

CHRISTMAS

Several listings offer Christmas getaways. If the information section indicates that the listing is open during the Christmas season, there is a very good chance that it offers a festive Christmas package.

CREDIT CARDS

The majority of places in this guide do not accept plastic payment. If the accommodation accepts payment by credit card, it is indicated using the terms AX—American Express, MC—MasterCard, VS—Visa, or simply, all major.

DIRECTIONS

We give concise driving directions to guide you to the listing which is often in a more out-of-the-way place than the town or village in the address. We would be very grateful if you would let us know of cases where our directions have proved inadequate.

ELECTRICITY

The voltage is 240. Most bathrooms have razor points (American-style) for 110 volts. It is recommended that overseas visitors take only dual voltage appliances and a kit of electrical plugs. Often your host can loan you a hairdryer or an iron.

Lower Slaughter

Introduction—About Bed and Breakfast Travel

MAPS

At the back of the book is a key map of Great Britain plus six regional maps showing the location of the town or village nearest the lodging. To make it easier for you, we have divided each location map into a grid of four parts, a, b, c, and d, as indicated on each map's key. The pertinent regional map number is given at the right on the top line of each bed and breakfast's description. These maps are an artist's renderings are not intended to replace commercial maps: our suggestion is to purchase a large-scale road atlas of England where an inch equals 10 miles. Our maps can be cross-referenced with those in our companion guide, *England, Wales & Scotland: Charming Hotels & Itineraries.*

MEALS

Prices quoted always include breakfast. Breakfast is most likely to be juice, a choice of porridge or cereal, followed by a plate of egg, bacon, sausage, tomatoes, and mushrooms completed by toast, marmalade, and jams. A great many places offer evening meals which should be requested at the time you make your reservation. You cannot expect to arrive at a bed and breakfast and receive dinner if you have not made reservations for it several days in advance. At some homes the social occasion of guests and host gathered around the dining-room table for an evening dinner party is a large part of the overall experience and many of these types of listings expect their guests to dine in. Places that do not offer evening meals are always happy to make recommendations for guests at nearby pubs or restaurants.

RATES

Rates are those quoted to us for the 1996 summer season. We have tried to standardize rates by quoting the 1996 per person bed-and-breakfast rate based on two people occupying a room. Not all places conform, so where dinner is included we have stated this in the listing. Prices are always quoted to include breakfast, Value Added Tax (VAT), and service (if these are applicable). Please use the figures printed as a guideline and be certain to ask what the rate is at the time of booking. Prices for a single are usually higher than the per-person rates and prices for a family room are sometimes lower. Many listings offer special terms, below their normal prices, for "short breaks" of two or more nights. In several listings suites are available at higher prices.

RESERVATIONS

Reservations can be confining and usually must be guaranteed by a deposit: however, if you have your heart set on a particular place, to avoid disappointment make a reservation. If you prefer to travel as whim and the weather dictate, rooms can often be had in the countryside with just a few days' notice. July and August are the busiest times and if you are traveling to a popular spot such as Bath or York, it is advisable to make reservations. It is completely unacceptable practice to make reservations for a particular night at several establishments, choosing at the last minute which one to stay at.

Although proprietors do not always strictly adhere to it, it is important to understand that once reservations are confirmed, whether by phone or in writing, you are under contract. This means that the proprietor is legally obligated to provide the accommodation he has promised and that you are bound to pay for that accommodation. If you cannot take up your accommodation, you are liable for a portion of the accommodation charges plus your deposit. If you have to cancel your reservation, do so as soon as possible so that the proprietor can attempt to re-let your room in which case you are liable only for the re-let fee or the deposit.

If you are visiting from overseas, our preference for making a reservation is by telephone: the cost is minimal and you have your answer immediately, so if space is not available, you can then decide on an alternate. If calling from the United States, allow for the time difference—England is five hours ahead of New York—so that you can call during their business day. Dial 011 (the international code), 44 (Britain's code), then the city code (dropping the 0), and the telephone number. Be specific as to what your needs are, such as a ground-floor room, en-suite bathroom, or twin beds. Check the prices which may well have changed from those given in the book (summer 1996). Ask what deposit to send or give your credit card number. Tell them about what time you intend to arrive and request dinner if you want it. Ask for a confirmation letter with brochure and map to be sent to you. Faxing is an excellent way to get a quick response in "black and white." In any written communication with England, do spell out the date since they reverse the American month/day numbering system—for example, to the English, 9/12 means December 9th, not September 12th.

SIGHTSEEING

We have tried to mention major sightseeing attractions near each lodging to encourage you to spend several nights in each location since few countries have as much to offer in a concentrated space as England. Within a few miles of every listing there are places of interest to visit and explore: lofty cathedrals, quaint churches, museums, and grand country houses.

SMOKING

Nearly all listings forbid smoking either in the bedrooms or public rooms. Some allow no smoking at all, in which case we state "No-smoking house." A list of no-smoking houses is at the back of the book. Ask about smoking policies if this is important to you—best to be forewarned rather than frustrated.

Polperro

SOCIALIZING

We have tried to indicate the degree of socializing that is included in your stay as some hosts treat their guests like visiting friends and relatives, sharing cocktails, eating with them around the dining room table, and joining them for coffee after dinner (the difference being that friends and relatives do not receive a bill at the end of their stay).

WOLSEY LODGES

Several of the listings are members of Wolsey Lodges, a consortium of private houses that open their doors to a handful of guests at a time. Visitors become a part of the household—guests are not expected to scuttle up to their rooms and family life does not carry on away from guests behind closed doors. Everyone usually dines together round a polished table, and unless you make special requests, you eat what is served to you. The conversation flows and you meet those you might never have met elsewhere. Early or late in the season, you may find that you are the only guests in these houses and you can enjoy a romantic candlelit dinner in a house full of character and charm. You are welcome as guests because you are the ones who help the owners pay their central heating bills, private school fees, and gardeners. As with all the listings in this guide, Wolsey Lodge members approach bed and breakfast in different ways—some are informal, while others offer a taste of refined, gracious living. If a lodging is a member of this group, we state "Wolsey Lodge" in the information section. A brochure listing all the Wolsey Lodge properties is available from Wolsey Lodges, 17 Chapel Street, Bildeston, Suffolk IP7 7EP, tel: (01449) 741297, fax: (01449) 741590. Places in this guide that are members of Wolsey Lodges are listed at the back of the book.

About England

DRIVING

Just about the time overseas visitors board their return flight home, they will have adjusted to driving on the "right" side which is the left side in England. You must contend with such things as roundabouts (circular intersections); flyovers (overpasses); ring roads (peripheral roads whose purpose is to bypass city traffic); lorries (trucks); laybies (turn outs); boots (trunks); and bonnets (hoods). Pedestrians are permitted to cross the road anywhere and always have the right of way. Seat belts must be worn at all times.

Motorways: The letter "M" precedes these convenient ways to cover long distances. With three lanes of traffic either side of a central divider, you should stay in the left-hand lane except for passing. Motorway exits are numbered and correspond to numbering on major road maps. Service areas supply petrol, cafeterias, and "bathrooms" (the word "bathroom" is used in the American sense—in Britain "bathroom" means a room with a shower or bathtub, not a toilet: "loo" is the most commonly used term for an American bathroom).

"A" Roads: The letter "A" precedes the road number. All major roads fall into this category. They vary from three lanes either side of a dividing barrier to single carriageways with an unbroken white line in the middle indicating that passing is not permitted. These roads have the rather alarming habit of changing from dual to single carriageway.

"B" Roads and Country Roads: The letter "B" preceding the road number or the lack of any lettering or numbering indicate that it belongs to the maze of country roads that crisscross Britain. These are the roads for people who have the luxury of time to enjoy the scenery en route. Arm yourself with a good map (although getting lost is part of the fun). Driving these narrow roads is terrifying at first but exhilarating after a while. Meandering down these roads, you can expect to spend time crawling behind a tractor or cows being herded to the farmyard. Some lanes are so narrow that there is room for only one car.

INFORMATION

The British Tourist Authority is an invaluable source of information. Their major offices are located as follows:

AUSTRALIA–SYDNEY: BTA, 210 Clarence Street, 8th Floor, Sydney, NSW 2000, tel: (02) 261 6034, fax: (02) 267 4442

CANADA–TORONTO: BTA, 111 Avenue Road, Suite 450, Toronto, Ontario M5R 3J8, tel: (416) 925-6326, fax: (416) 961-2175

FRANCE–PARIS: BTA, Maison de la Grand Bretagne, 19 Rue des Mathurins, 75009 Paris, tel: (1) 4451 5620, fax: (1) 4451 5621

GERMANY–FRANKFURT: BTA, Taunusstrasse 52-60, 60329 Frankfurt, tel: (069) 238 0711, fax: (069) 238 0717

NEW ZEALAND–AUCKLAND: BTA, Suite 305, 3rd Floor, Dilworth Building, corner Queen and Customs Streets, Auckland, tel: (09) 303 1446, fax: (09) 377 6965

USA–CHICAGO: BTA, 625 North Michigan Avenue, Suite 1510, Chicago, IL 60611— walk-in enquiries only

USA–NEW YORK: BTA, 551 Fifth Avenue, New York, NY 10176, tel: (800) 462-2748 or in NY (212) 986-2200.

If you need additional information while you are in Britain, there are more than 700 official Tourist Information Centers identified by a blue-and-white letter "I" and "Tourist Information" signs. Many information centers will make reservations for local accommodation and larger ones will "book a bed ahead" in a different locality.

In London at the British Travel Center at 4–12 Lower Regent Street, London SW1 (near Piccadilly Circus tube station) you can book a room, buy air or train tickets, hire a car or pay for a coach tour or theatre tickets. The center also has exhibitions and films. It is open 9 am to 6:30 pm, Monday to Saturday; 10 am to 4 pm on Sunday.

PUBS

Pubs are a British institution. Traditional pubs with inviting names such as the Red Lion, Wheatsheaf, and King's Arms are found at the heart of every village. Not only are they a great place to meet the locals over a pint or a game of dominoes or darts, but they offer an inviting place to dine. Food served in the bar enables you to enjoy an inexpensive meal while sipping your drink in convivial surroundings. Bar meals range from a bowl of soup to a delicious cooked dinner. Many pubs have dining rooms that serve more elaborate fare in equally convivial but more sophisticated surroundings. The key to success when dining at a pub is to obtain a recommendation from where you are staying that night—your host is always happy to assist you.

Kersey

Introduction—About England

SHOPPING

Overseas visitors can reclaim the VAT (Value Added Tax) paid on the goods they purchase. Not all stores participate in the refund scheme and there is often a minimum purchase price. Stores that do participate will ask to see your passport before completing the VAT form which must be presented with the goods to the Customs officer at the point of departure from Britain within three months of purchase. The customs officer will certify the form which you return to the store where you bought the goods. The store will then send you a check in sterling for the refund.

SIGHTSEEING

There is so much to see in every little nook and cranny of England: cottage gardens, Roman ruins, stately homes, thatched villages, ancient castles, Norman churches, smugglers' inns, bluebell woods, historic manors, museums on every subject. All set in a land that moves from wild moorland to verdant farmland, woodland to meadow, vast sand beaches to rugged cliffs. Most sightseeing venues operate a summer and a winter opening schedule, the changeover occurring around late March/early April and late October/early November. Before you embark on an excursion, check the dates and hours of opening. The British Tourist Office is an invaluable resource for what to see and do in an area. Our companion guide, *England, Wales & Scotland: Charming Hotels & Itineraries,* includes countryside driving itineraries which are useful in helping you plan your holiday.

Introduction—About England

WEATHER

Britain has a tendency to be moist at all times of the year. The cold in winter is rarely severe; however, the farther north you go, the greater the possibility of being snowed in. Spring can be wet, but it is a lovely time to travel—the summer crowds have not descended, daffodils and bluebells fill the woodlands, and the hedgerows are full of wildflowers. Summer offers the best chance of sunshine, but also the largest crowds. Schools are usually closed the last two weeks of July and all of August, so this is the time when most families take their summer holidays. Travel is especially hectic on the weekends in summer—try to avoid major routes and airports at these times. Autumn is also an ideal touring time. The weather tends to be drier than in spring and the woodlands are decked in their golden autumn finery.

Scotney Castle

Introduction—About England

Places to Stay

We found Judith and David Pritchard busy in the garden and kitchen picking blackcurrants and redcurrants and cooking them into jams and jellies. As we accompanied them through their fruit and vegetable garden we realized why they have no time for the swimming pool, the sauna, or the tennis court—the garden and the care of their guests is a full-time occupation. The Pritchards' easy, friendly manner soon has you feeling at home. While guests are welcome to use the large formal drawing room, they often prefer to sit cozily by the fire in the hall parlor. Judith is happy to prepare dinner, and guests are usually served at separate tables. Upstairs, the most spacious bedroom is Mogul (named for the Indian prints that hang upon the flowery wallpaper) which has a full bathroom and a separate shower. In addition there is another double bedroom and a small single room that can accommodate a child. Fly-fishing folk enjoy fishing the nearby Rivers Test, Avon, and Itchen. Salisbury and Winchester are within easy reach as are Broadlands (the late Lord Mountbatten's home at Romsey) and Highclere Castle with its Egyptian treasures. *Directions:* From the A303 (near Andover) take the A343, Salisbury road, and take the first right turn down a very narrow, unmarked lane: Abbotts Law is the third house on the right. (The lane is just before a thatched cottage and almost opposite a trout farm.)

ABBOTTS LAW
Owners: Judith & David Pritchard
Abbotts Ann
Andover
Hampshire SPA 7DW, England
Tel & fax: (01264) 710350
2 rooms, 1 en suite
From £25 per person
Open April to October
Children over 5

The Old Vicarage offers visitors an exceptionally delightful place to stay in this tranquil part of the country immortalized in Thomas Hardy's novels. Standing next to the old village church, surrounded by green lawns, neatly clipped hedges, and rose gardens, this fine Georgian house is owned by Anthea and Michael Hipwell who, along with their black labrador Beeze, offer a warm welcome to their gracious home. Breakfast is the only meal that Anthea prepares, but she has a long list of wonderful restaurants in the surrounding villages. Upstairs, the bedrooms have pretty wallpapers and are furnished in tasteful English country style, in character with the decor throughout The Old Vicarage. There is a lot to see and do in the area: Cerne Abbas with its thatched cottage and giant carved into the hillside is the Casterbridge of Hardy's novels, and historic Dorchester, Salisbury, and Shaftesbury are nearby. The Dorset coast (Lulworth Cove, Durdle Door, and Ringstead Bay) is a 20-minute drive. *Directions:* From Dorchester take the A35 northeast for 5 miles to Tolpuddle (this is the village where the six martyrs met to fight starvation farmworkers' wages) where you turn right for Affpuddle (1 mile).

THE OLD VICARAGE
Owners: Anthea & Michael Hipwell
Affpuddle
Dorchester
Dorset DT2 7HH, England
Tel: (01305) 848315
3 rooms, 2 en suite
From £21 per person
Open all year
Children over 12

Sheila and Tony Sutton have converted this impressive house, which was built as a vicarage in 1869, into a small hotel providing a centrally located, comfortable, hospitable base for exploring the Lake District. Bric-a-brac, capacious sofas, and an aspidistra in the window give a cluttered, Victorian air to the front lounge, though I would term the overall decor comfortably eclectic. Accommodation can be taken on a bed and breakfast basis, but guests usually opt for the dinner, bed and breakfast rate because the Suttons make every effort to make dinner a special occasion. A typical menu might include warm smoked trout mousse with watercress and lemon, guinea fowl with walnuts and mushrooms, sticky toffee pudding, and cheese. Grey Friar is just a short distance from the bustling center of Ambleside. Whether you explore Lakeland by car or on foot, you will find the scenery glorious: in spring the famous daffodils bloom, while in autumn the bracken and leaves turn a crisp, golden brown. At nearby Grasmere are Rydal Mount and Dove Cottage, poet William Wordsworth's homes. Hawkshead has a museum honoring Beatrix Potter and in Near Sawrey you can visit her home, Hill Top Farm, where she dreamed up such endearing characters as Mrs Tiggy Winkle and the Flopsy Bunnies. *Directions:* Grey Friar Lodge is 1½ miles west of Ambleside on the A593, midway between Ambleside and Skelwith Bridge.

GREY FRIAR LODGE
Owners: Sheila & Tony Sutton
Clappersgate
Ambleside
Cumbria LA22 9NE, England
Tel & fax: (015394) 33158
8 rooms, 7 en suite
From £23.50 per person
Open March to October
Children over 12

Waterton Garden Cottage is part of a Victorian stable block that has been cleverly converted to two spacious homes. The house is set in a red-brick, walled garden of spacious lawns and flower beds with a heated swimming pool occupying a quiet corner beyond espaliered fruit trees. Ian, who has over 40 years experience in catering and hospitality, and his wife, Mary, work as a team preparing dinner with Ian responsible for the main course and Mary concentrating on dessert. Guests are encouraged to bring their own wine to accompany the meal. What was once the tack-room is now a paneled dining room hung with framed photographs of tempting food dishes. A narrow, spiral staircase leads up to the guests' bedrooms (larger suitcases are not a problem as Ian transports them via the main staircase). Bedrooms are prettily decorated and each is accompanied by a modern, en-suite shower room. If you care for tea or coffee, just ask and it will be served to you in the drawing room. Waterton Garden Cottage is a quiet countryside spot where a short drive will bring you to the heart of Cirencester. Southern Cotswold villages such as Bibury with its beautiful old cottages are within easy reach. *Directions:* From Cirencester take the A417 (Lechlade road) for 2½ miles to Ampney Crucis. Turn right before the Crown of Crucis Hotel, signposted Driffield. Take the first farm track to the right and Waterton Garden Cottage is at the end (do not pull into the courtyard).

WATERTON GARDEN COTTAGE
Owners: Mary & Ian Cassidy
Ampney Crucis
Gloucestershire GL7 5RX, England
Tel: (01285) 851303
3 en-suite rooms
From £22.50 per person
Closed Christmas
Children over 9
No-smoking house

Whenever Elizabeth or Peter Hartland see people peering curiously up their driveway they know they're Richmonds looking for their roots, for Cove House was the home of John Richmond who went with the men of Taunton to found Taunton, Massachusetts, in 1640. The Richmonds belong to the Richmond Society, a group who can trace their ancestors back to this wisteria-festooned manor house. Guests enjoy breakfast in the gracious dining room where lovely flower arrangements dress antique furniture. In the small adjacent study, an alcove lined with a detailed map of the area illustrates the many places of interest round and about: Avebury, Blenheim Palace, Oxford, Bath, and the Cotswold villages. The bedrooms are large and some can take an extra child's bed and cot. Nearby, flooded gravel pits which attract many species of waterfowl provide a birdwatcher's paradise. Peter, a retired schoolmaster, keeps informational brochures on hand for visitors' use and has also compiled a "good food guide" to local pubs and restaurants. Guests often walk the short distance into the village to eat at the White Hart or the Horse and Jockey. With advance notice, Elizabeth is happy to prepare an evening meal for guests. *Directions:* The village of Ashton Keynes is 6 miles south of Cirencester. In the center of the village is the White Hart and 100 yards east a large wall bounds the driveway to Cove House. Drive through the inner gate.

COVE HOUSE
Owners: Elizabeth & Peter Hartland
2 Cove House
Ashton Keynes
Wiltshire SN6 6NS, England
Tel: (01285) 861221
3 en-suite rooms
From £24 per person
Closed Christmas
Children welcome
Wolsey Lodge

Austwick is a delightful village with a pub, post office-cum-general store, church, and a cluster of houses set against the background of the rolling limestone hills in the Three Peaks area of the Yorkshire Dales National Park. Just at the edge of the village green, Wood View, one of the village's larger houses, is home to Pam and Peter Taylor who used to run a nearby hotel before moving here. Their front door opens to a welcoming fire in the sitting room, just perfect for toasting your toes after a long day walking across the fells. Breakfast is the only meal served at the little tables in the low-beamed dining room and, while there's a pub next door, guests often dine at the Cross Streets pub just a short drive away. The bedrooms are delightfully decorated in a very pleasing, unfussy way. I especially admired the two large front bedrooms and the attic bedroom with its massive support beam which tall folks have to duck under. The Settle to Carlisle railway is a great local attraction and Pam recommends that guests take the train as far as Appelby, where the gypsies hold their horse fair every June. Within an hour's leisurely drive you can be in the Lake District, the Trough of Bowland, Bronte Country, and the heart of the Yorkshire dales. *Directions:* Driving from Skipton towards Kendal on the A65, turn right into Austwick village which is 4½ miles beyond Settle. Wood View is in the center of the village by the green.

WOOD VIEW
Owners: Pam & Peter Taylor
The Green
Austwick
Lancaster LA2 8BB, England
Tel: (015242) 51268
5 en-suite rooms
From £18 per person
Open Easter to October
Children over 5

The Barns is a comfortable spot to break a long journey between London and Edinburgh via the A1, or for a longer visit to explore Nottinghamshire. This county is famous not only for the exploits of Robin Hood, but also as the area where the Pilgrim Fathers formed their separatist church before setting sail for America and establishing a new colony. The Barns is the very tastefully converted hay and tractor barns of the next-door farm, and behind its red-brick facade all is spick and span. A sofa and chairs are drawn around a crackling log fire, and tables are topped with linen cloths neatly laid for breakfast. With advance notice, Rosalie is happy to cook a traditional roast dinner. Upstairs the bedrooms are plainly decorated with cream walls highlighting dark beams and all have nice touches such as a fresh posy of flowers on a small antique dresser and elegant china tea cups. Room 1 is a particularly large family suite. A pleasant drive through Sherwood Forest brings visitors to the visitors' center which has an exhibition on Robin Hood and his merry band and offers maps guiding you through ancient oak trees to his former hideaways. Clumber Park near Sherwood Forest is noted for its main driveway planted with over 1,296 lime trees. *Directions:* From the south take the A1 north to the A57 (Worksop) roundabout, make a U turn and go south on the A1. Take the first left, on the B6420, towards Retford. The Barns is on the left.

THE BARNS
Owner: Rosalie Brammer
Morton Farm
Babworth, Retford
Nottinghamshire DN22 8HA, England
Tel: (01777) 706336
6 en-suite rooms
From £20 per person
Closed Christmas
Credit cards: all major
Children welcome

On a road of large, semi-detached Edwardian homes, Haydon House distinguishes itself as having the most colorful, pocket-sized garden. Magdalene has made the most of her home, decorating each of the rooms to perfection. Guests enjoy the sitting room with its plump sofas drawn cozily round the fire or the pocket-sized study with just enough room to spread your maps and books to plan the next day's adventures. The bedrooms are exceedingly pretty and named for the color of their decor: strawberry, gooseberry, blueberry, elderberry, and mulberry. Request blueberry or elderberry if you want a more spacious room. Mulberry, tucked under the eaves, is an especially attractive triple or family room. With a choice of over 90 restaurants in the town, breakfast is the only meal served and includes a fresh fruit platter and several other alternatives to a traditional, cooked English breakfast. Bath with its graceful, honey-colored buildings, interesting museums, and superb shopping merits several days of exploration. *Directions:* From Bath follow signs onto the A367 towards Exeter, pass an elongated roundabout by a railway viaduct, up a hill to a small shopping area, and onto a dual carriageway (The Bear pub is on your right). At the end of the shopping area fork right into Bloomfield Road and take the second right (by the telephone kiosk) into Bloomfield Park.

HAYDON HOUSE
Owners: Magdalene & Gordon Ashman-Marr
9 Bloomfield Park
Bath
Avon BA2 2BY, England
Tel & fax: (01225) 444919/427351
5 en-suite rooms
From £27.50 per person
Open all year
Credit cards: all major
Children welcome
No-smoking house

Perched high above the city's rooftops, this large Victorian home offers every comfort for the visitor: luxurious bathrooms with heated towel rails and "perfect" showers, firm, American queen-sized beds, satellite television, in-house movies, picture-perfect decor, and the sincere attentions of George. Each of the bedrooms has its own flavor and, while I admired those in soft flowery pastels (the pink tower room with its lacy four-poster bed is very popular with honeymooners and there is a spacious ground-floor room for those who have difficulty with stairs), I particularly enjoyed the imaginative four-poster room where four turquoise obelisks are artfully draped in navy and white fabric to form the bedposts of this most interesting bed. Breakfast in the sunny green and yellow breakfast room offers lots of choices as well as the traditional English cooked breakfast. It's a 15-minute walk down into town. George has designed day-long driving tours with detailed instructions for a full day's sightseeing, so guests often venture as far afield as southern Wales. *Directions:* From Bath follows signs onto the A367 towards Exeter, pass an elongated roundabout by a railway viaduct, go up a hill, and take the first turning to the right into Upper Oldfield Park. Holly Lodge is the first house on the right just past the bend.

HOLLY LODGE
Owner: George Hall
8 Upper Oldfield Park
Bath
Avon BA2 3JZ, England
Tel: (01225) 424042/339187 Fax: (01225) 481138
7 en-suite rooms
From £37.50 per person
Open all year
Credit cards: all major
Children welcome
No-smoking house

Situated halfway up a steep hill, Somerset House is a classic Regency abode of warm, honey-colored stone, set in a spacious garden affording panoramic views of the city. The family pets (a parrot, dog, and cat), along with family photos and books give a comfortable feeling to the Seymours' upscale guesthouse. Decorated in pastels, the bedrooms have matching drapes and bedspreads and whimsical rag dolls propped up on the pillows. Several rooms have an extra bed and a ground-floor room is ideal for those who have difficulty with stairs. Bedrooms are named after the sons and daughters of George III and in their note to guests Jean and Malcolm have included the child's historical particulars as well as the rules of the house. Jean and Jonathan specialize in delicious regional English cuisine. Saturday nights (not in the summer) are particularly special, for Jean plans a theme meal (on the night of our stay it was France), and gives a verbal rendition of the menu, explaining the origins of the dishes and their tempting contents. The basement dining room complements the food: light-wood Windsor chairs, lace-topped tables, and a huge pine dresser set upon the checkerboard tile floor. A 15-minute walk brings you into the heart of Bath. *Directions:* Do not go into the city center, but follow signs for the university. Going up Bathwick Hill, Somerset House is on the left.

SOMERSET HOUSE
Owners: Jean, Malcolm, & Jonathan Seymour
35 Bathwick Hill
Bath
Avon BA2 6LD, England
Tel: (01225) 466451/463471 Fax: (01225) 317188
10 rooms, 9 en suite
From £31.00 per person
Open all year
Children over 10
No-smoking house

This listed Georgian country house is one of the many lovely homes in the conservation village of Bathford. The Orchard is set in its own walled grounds which feature sweeping lawns and a magnificent variety of old trees. It is difficult to believe that the bustling city of Bath is just 15 minutes away from this tranquil spot. Olga and John London have a winning formula of a handsome house in beautiful surroundings, immaculately decorated and furnished with a tasteful mixture of fine antiques. Guests have full use of a very elegant yet very welcoming sitting room where a log fire blazes on chilly evenings and tall French doors and a large window open up to views of the perfectly groomed garden. Upstairs are three very generously proportioned, high ceilinged bedrooms with large bay windows, discreetly placed televisions, and spacious bathrooms. The two front bedrooms have enviable views of an enormous copper beech tree, reputedly over 200 years old, and across the valley to green fields. The fourth bedroom, nicknamed The Folly, has a private garden entrance, lower ceilings, and small windows that overlook the garden. Guests who enjoy a country walk are directed across the orchard the nature reserve. Most guests stroll down the hill to dine at The Crown Inn. *Directions:* Leave the M4 at junction 18 and follow the A46 south to the A4 (towards Chippenham), turn right onto the A363 and left, at The Crown Inn, into Bathford. The Orchard is up the hill on the right, 200 yards beyond Bathford Post Office

THE ORCHARD
Owners: Olga & John London
Bathford
Bath
Avon BA1 7TG, England
Tel: (01225) 858765
4 rooms, 3 en suite
From £28.50 per person
Open March to October
Children over 12

Frog Street Farm, a lovely gray-stone farmhouse dating back to 1436, is a real working farm where things are not fancy or cutesy pretty, but everything fits together perfectly with country freshness. From the moment you are met at the door by Veronica, with her true country-style warmth and jolly sense of humor, the mood is set. You are immediately made to feel part of the family and offered a cup of tea in front of the large inglenook fireplace before being shown to your room. The guestrooms are spotlessly clean and simply, but prettily, decorated with a color scheme of pinks and greens used throughout. Behind the house lies the farmyard while to the front is a colorful garden and a swimming pool shaded by a tall hedge. Veronica takes great pride in her cooking and, with advance notice, will prepare delicious meals from farm-fresh produce. For those who want to spend a few days in the country, away from city sophistication, Frog Street Farm is the epitome of what a farm vacation should be. In this pretty, rolling countryside are the charming little towns of Chard, Ilchester, Ilminster, and Crewkerne. To the north the limestone Mendip Hills are honeycombed with spectacular caves and gorges such as Wookey Hole and Cheddar Gorge. The magnificent cathedral city of Wells is within easy driving distance. *Directions:* From the M5 take exit 25 and continue 4½ miles southeast to Hatch Beauchamp. Take Station Road to Frog Street Farm.

FROG STREET FARM
Owner: Veronica Cole
Beercrocombe
Taunton
Somerset TA3 6AF, England
Tel: (01823) 480430
3 en-suite rooms
From £25 per person
Open March to October
Children over 12

Sue and John Bruder's home is a classic Georgian country house, decorated in period style, in the heart of the Kentish countryside. John Bruder was a banker in Zambia, where his wife Sue had a career in computer programming and a passion for gourmet cooking. When the Bruders returned to England they bought Crit Hall and realized their ambition to own a small country house with first-class accommodation and food. Guests enjoy the contrast of a formal four-course dinner in the evening in the dining room and an informal breakfast in the spacious country kitchen where Sue prepares breakfast on the Aga under a beamed ceiling hung with hops and chats to guests about their plans for the day. The bedrooms have extremely pleasing, smartly tailored decor with taffeta draperies and bedspreads and antique furniture. Two have their bathrooms en suite while the third has its private bathroom next door. Popular touring destinations are the gardens of Sissinghurst and Scotney Castle, the squat fortress of Bodiam Castle, moated Hever Castle, the cobbled streets of Rye, and Canterbury with its magnificent cathedral. *Directions:* From Cranbrook take the A229 towards Hawkhurst. Turn left on the B2086 towards Benenden and Crit Hall is on your right after 2 miles.

CRIT HALL   **NEW**
Owners: Sue & John Bruder
Cranbrook Road
Benenden
Kent TN17 4EU, England
Tel: (01580) 240609 Fax: (01580) 241743
3 rooms, 2 en suite
From £24 per person
Closed mid-December to mid-January
Credit cards: MC, VS
Children over 10

I cannot guarantee that Drummond will take you for a ride on his miniature train, but you might be lucky enough to take the ¼-mile circuit of the 6-acre garden, past the front door, through a long tunnel, and past the heated swimming pool. This makes Birchley seem like a theme park which it most certainly is not: it's a spectacular Tudor home whose former owners had visions of grandeur when they tacked on an enormous Edwardian addition which is now the house next door. There are three simply wonderful bedrooms, two with snug shower rooms and one with an enormous bath. Guests toast their toes in front of the log fire in the snug, oak-paneled sitting room and enjoy a hearty breakfast served on an ancient refectory table in the massive oak-beamed dining room with its glorious, carved oak inglenook. There are excellent pubs and restaurants within a few minutes' drive. This superb house merits a stay of several days—you can spend a week just touring gardens. Churchill's home, Chartwell, gives you a glimpse into the life of one of Britain's most famous politicians. Rye, Hastings, Dover, and Canterbury are popular destinations. *Directions:* Leave the M20 at junction 8 following signs for Leeds Castle. In 4 miles turn left at the Plough Inn in the direction of Tenterden. After 6 miles, turn right at the green in Biddenden (Tunbridge Wells), and after 1 mile turn left (opposite the garden center) and Birchley is on your left.

BIRCHLEY
Owners: Jennifer & Drummond Randall
Fosten Green Lane
Biddenden, Ashford
Kent TH27 8DZ, England
Tel: (01580) 291413 Fax: (01580) 291413
3 en-suite rooms
From £30 per person
Closed December to mid-January
Children over 12

In the last century the owners of River Hall bought Biddenden's ancient market hall, moved it to their estate, and used it as a coach house. More recent occupants decided to incorporate the market hall into a traditional home. The sitting room was formerly the beamed market where farmers once sold their produce and upstairs the village meeting hall is the principal guest bedroom. An additional twin-bedded room—small only by comparison to its beamed neighbor—has a smart en-suite bathroom while the beamed bedroom's bathroom is large enough to accommodate both a bath and a separate shower. With advance notice, Sara is happy to provide a light supper or a three- or four-course dinner, whichever is required. The Sleighs are also glad to recommend restaurants and pubs round and about for dinner. In the morning guests make their way through the kitchen to enjoy breakfast in the conservatory which overlooks the sheltered garden. Within easy reach are the famous gardens of Sissinghurst and Great Dixter, the castles of Hever, Leeds, Scotney, and Bodiam, and the delightful cobbled streets of Rye. Farther afield lie Canterbury and Royal Tunbridge Wells. *Directions:* From Biddenden take the A262 towards Tenterden and take the first left-hand turn down a country road for about a mile to a T-junction. Turn left and River Hall Coach House is on your right.

RIVER HALL COACH HOUSE   **NEW**
Owners: Sara & Bill Sleigh
Biddenden
Kent TN27 8JE, England
Tel: (01580) 291565 Fax: (01580) 292137
2 en-suite rooms
From £26 per person
Closed Christmas
Children over 12
No-smoking house

This well proportioned Victorian rectory is set in secluded grounds overlooking glorious vistas of the Derbyshire countryside. Geraldine and Stuart Worthington's solicitous welcome includes an invitation to the evening dinner party. Guests are introduced to each other over cocktails in the drawing room before sitting down to the large dining-room table, beautifully laid with silver and crystal. Geraldine and Stuart dine with their guests; Geraldine serving unobtrusively, with Stuart pouring the wine. After dinner, guests, host, and hostess return to the drawing room for port and coffee around the cheery log fire. The front bedroom has a large double bed framed by blue-and-white flowered draperies hung from a coronet, matching bedspread and bed ruffle, and an en-suite bathroom. The large twin room has thick bathrobes so guests can pop comfortably across the hall to their bathroom. The third twin room tucked under the eaves has a steeply sloping ceiling and adjacent luxurious shower room. The dramatic and rugged Derbyshire scenery is a strong attraction for walkers. Many visitors also tour Chatsworth House, Haddon Hall, and the open-air Monday market in Bakewell. *Directions:* Leave Ashbourne on the A52 towards Leek. After 2 miles turn right towards Ilam. Drive through Okeover Park and turn left as you go through the gates. After 2 miles, at Blore crossroads, turn left and The Old Rectory is on your right beyond the church.

THE OLD RECTORY
Owners: Geraldine & Stuart Worthington
Blore, Ashbourne
Derbyshire DE CBS, England
Tel & fax: (01335) 350287
3 rooms, 1 en suite
From £35 per person
Closed Christmas
Credit cards: MC, VS
Children not accepted
Wolsey Lodge

With its back nestled against woodland, Boldre Hill faces out across rolling countryside to the distant coast and the Isle of Wight. Spacious, high-ceilinged rooms and broad hallways characterize this large home where Anna Morris, in the Wolsey Lodge tradition, welcomes guests as friends. On chilly days the fire in the drawing room provides a cheery warmth. In summer, guests often relax under the wisteria on the terrace. Guests dine together round a lovely old table that fits snugly at one end of the dining room, leaving plenty of room for sofas and a television at the other. The principal bedroom enjoys a large bathroom and a huge bay window which frames the countryside view. Two very attractive, twin-bedded rooms face the woodlands at the rear of the house. Just up the lane there's walking, riding, and pony-watching in the New Forest. The sea is close by with lovely walks along the beaches. A ferry sails from nearby Lymington to the Isle of Wight. If you are interested in cars, be sure to visit the world-famous motor museum at Beaulieu. *Directions:* From Bockenhurst railway crossing, on the A337, continue for 2½ miles towards Lymington, turn left at the signpost for Boldre and Pilley (not the turning to Boldre church), and Boldre Hill is on your right, opposite the entrance to Hill House School.

BOLDRE HILL
Owner: Anna Morris
Rope Hill
Boldre
Lymington
Hampshire SO41 8ND, England
Tel: (01590) 672614
3 en-suite rooms
From £30 per person
Closed Christmas
Children welcome
Wolsey Lodge

Kath and Tony Peacock enjoy nothing more than singing with their church choir which is so noted for its musical prowess that it travels to Europe and America to give concerts. How appropriate with their ecclesiastical connection that they live in what was Boltongate's large, rambling, Victorian rectory. Tony loves to cook and stays busy in the kitchen while Kath has pre-dinner drinks with guests in the colorfully decorated drawing room. In contrast to the other tall-ceilinged, large-windowed rooms of the rectory, the dining room dates back to the 16th century and has a low beamed ceiling and a large inglenook fireplace with a wood-burning stove. Here guests dine together by lamplight, feasting on Anthony's specialties. Bedrooms are large and comfortable, decorated with pretty wallpapers and matching drapes. Two have en-suite bathrooms while the largest has its bathroom (robes provided) down the hall. Boltongate is on the quiet, northernmost fringes of the Lake District, a perfect spot to break a journey to or from Scotland. Pretty towns and villages abound such as Caldbeck, Borrowdale, Ullswater, and Buttermere. William Wordsworth's birthplace is nearby in Cockermouth. *Directions:* Leave the M6 at exit 40, bypass Keswick and take the A591 for 7 miles. At the Castle Inn turn right at the sign for Ireby. Boltongate Old Rectory is the first house in the village on your right.

BOLTONGATE OLD RECTORY
Owners: Kathleen & Anthony Peacock
Boltongate
Cumbria CA5 1DA, England
Tel: (016973) 71647 Fax: (016973) 71798
3 rooms, 2 en suite
From £33.50 per person
Closed December
Credit cards: MC, VS
Children over 14
No-smoking house
Wolsey Lodge

Visitors come to Pethills Bank Cottage to visit the sights in the region, then return because this bed and breakfast is the most delightful place to stay. Set high on a hill surrounded by fields, the cottage sits snug in an acre of rolling gardens overlooking the countryside. The cozy living room has thick, golden-stone walls and a large picture window framing the rolling lawn and rockery garden. The bedrooms are unexpectedly large, decorated in an unobtrusive, modern style which gives them a light, airy, and uncluttered feel. Each has an en-suite bathroom and a host of extras: biscuit jar brimming with tempting goodies, fruit bowl, mineral water, iron, hairdryer, remote-control television, shampoo, and bath oil. The Garden Room, decorated in pretty greens and creams, opens up to a verandah which overlooks the fields, The Dales Room also has magnificent countryside views and the largest bathroom. The Cottage Room has old-world charm with a beamed ceiling and low windows. Breakfast fortifies you for the entire day as it includes an array of fruits, crisp bacon, sausage, eggs, tomatoes, and mushrooms, and toast with homemade jam and marmalade. Yvonne helps guests plan visits to the Potteries factories and seconds shops (for example, Coalport, Royal Doulton, Minton, Spode, and Wedgwood). Derbyshire's dales and historic houses are close at hand. *Directions:* Bottomhouse is on the A523 between Leek and Ashbourne. Turn into the lane opposite the Little Chef restaurant and follow the signs up the hill for about a mile.

PETHILLS BANK COTTAGE
Owners: Yvonne & Richard Martin
Bottomhouse, Leek
Staffordshire ST13 7PF, England
Tel: (01538) 304277/304555 Fax: (01538) 304575
3 en-suite rooms
From £19.50 per person
Closed Christmas to March
Children welcome

This exquisite home takes its name from the Bourne Eau stream which runs alongside its grounds, separating it from an ancient abbey and a park. This house has evolved over the years and Dawn and George Bishop have decorated each room according to its historical period. The Elizabethan dining room has a flagstone floor topped with an Oriental carpet and a trestle table set before a huge inglenook fireplace beneath a low beamed ceiling. The high-ceilinged, formal Georgian drawing room has enviable antiques and the snug Jacobean music room has a concert piano and a cheery log fire blazing in the ornately carved fireplace. Guests enjoy a scrumptious cooked breakfast in the low-ceilinged breakfast room furnished in mellow country pine. Bedrooms are equally lovely: the enormous Master Suite has a large sitting area around a fireplace whose mantle was once part of the abbey's altar and an adjacent dressing room with a single bed; the smaller Jacobean Room with its period bed has a glorious modern bathroom; and the large twin-bedded Georgian Room has a private staircase and views across the vast lawns. Many guests visit Burghley House, Belton House, Belvoir Castle, Grimsthorpe Castle, and Stamford where the film *Middlemarch* was filmed. Gently rolling wolds lead north to Lincoln with its cobbled streets, majestic hilltop cathedral, and castle. *Directions:* Bourne is on the A15 between Peterborough and Sleaford. The concealed entrance is on the A15, 200 yards south of the main traffic lights in the middle of town, opposite the park.

BOURNE EAU HOUSE
Owners: Dawn & George Bishop
Bourne
Lincolnshire PE10 9LY, England
Tel: (01778) 423621
3 en-suite rooms
From £30 per person
Closed Christmas and Easter
Children welcome
Wolsey Lodge

Deep in the Dorset countryside on the beautiful Isle of Purbeck, a farm track leads you to Bucknowle House which sits amongst rolling hills. The Victorians believed in spacious domestic architecture and as a consequence most of Bucknowle's rooms are large and all have high ceilings. Sara and Richard Harvey have papered the dining room in a pretty blue paper accented with gold stars and it is here that guests breakfast together around the large table. A family portrait of Sara, Richard, and their three sons hangs in the guest sitting room with its comfortable sofa and chairs drawn round the fireplace. Up the broad staircase the three homelike bedrooms are named after their color schemes: green, pink, and blue. All have attractive decor and fabrics that coordinate with the painted walls. All around you are quiet country lanes weaving through the Purbeck Hills to pretty villages. Interesting places to visit include the dramatic ruins of Corfe Castle, the sheltered bay of Lulworth Cove, the Arne Heath nature reserve, the old-fashioned resort of Swanage, the interesting town of Wareham whose roads were laid out by the Romans, Bournemouth, and the army tank museum at Bovington. *Directions:* From Wareham take the Swanage road (A351). Approaching Corfe Castle (4 miles), turn right immediately underneath the ruins, signposted to Church Knowle. A track on the left after half a mile is signposted for Bucknowle House.

BUCKNOWLE HOUSE   **NEW**
Owners: Sara & Richard Harvey
Bucknowle, Wareham
Dorset BH20 5PO, England
Tel: (01929) 480352 Fax: (01929) 481275
3 en-suite rooms
From £25 per person
Open all year
Children welcome

Pickett Howe is a picture-perfect, whitewashed farmhouse nestled amongst green fields beneath rugged Lakeland peaks. As you drive into the farmyard, Rowan, a golden retriever, greets you with enthusiastic tail-wagging and smiles. And, best of all, the interior lives up to all the promise of the exterior: there are polished slate floors topped with Oriental rugs, heavy oak beams, and small stone-mullioned windows set deep in thick stone walls. Sitting on the sofa chatting with Dani and David over tea and homemade cakes, you soon feel thoroughly at home. Upstairs, the four little bedrooms tucked neatly under the eaves have Victorian brass-and-wrought-iron beds, three have Jacuzzi bathtubs (and showers), while the fourth has a shower. Dani loves to cook and produces sumptuous dinners where there is always a choice of meat, fish, or vegetarian for the main course: small wonder that rigorous walking is often the order of the day. Dani and David were the national winners of the coveted English Tourist Board's "England for Excellence" award in 1994. Meander across Brackenthwaite Howe to sit quietly by Crummock Water (the Edwards have the National Trust boathouse key) or stride up Grasmoor. *Directions:* From exit 40 on the M6 take the A66 past Keswick, turn left onto the B5292 to Lorton, then follow signs for Buttermere. After 2 miles take the left fork (B5289) for Buttermere and the entrance to Pickett Howe is on your right after 1/3 mile.

PICKETT HOWE
Owners: Dani & David Edwards
Brackenthwaite, Buttermere Valley
Cumbria CA13 9UY, England
Tel: (01900) 85444
4 en-suite rooms
From £36 per person
Open April to mid-November
Credit cards: MC, VS
Children over 10
No-smoking house

Priory Steps, a row of 17th-century weavers' cottages high above the town of Bradford on Avon, is a glorious place to stay. The village tumbles down the hill to the banks of the River Avon, its narrow streets full of interesting shops and antique dealers. A few miles distant, the glories of Bath await exploration and are easily accessible by car or the local train service. Hostess Diana is a gourmet cook and guests dine *en famille* in the traditionally furnished dining room. While Diana's cooking is reason enough to spend several days here, the adjacent library with its books and pamphlets highlighting the many places to visit in the area provides additional justification. The bedrooms are all very different, each accented with antique furniture, and each has a smart modern bathroom, television, and tea and coffee tray. The Blue Room has large shuttered and curtained windows and a pleasing decor in shades of blue, while the large English Room has striped paper in muted tones of green coordinating with flowered curtains. There is a touch of whimsy in the bathroom of the dark-beamed Frog Room where the odd frog or two has inspired former guests to send their own contributions to an ever-growing collection of the creatures. The frogless bedroom itself is very pretty. *Directions:* Take the A363 from Bath to Bradford on Avon. As the road drops steeply into the town, Newtown is the first road to the right. Priory Steps is 150 yards on the left.

PRIORY STEPS
Owners: Diana & Carey Chapman
Newtown
Bradford on Avon
Wiltshire BA15 1NQ, England
Tel: (01225) 862230 Fax: (01225) 866248
5 en-suite rooms
From £29 per person
Open all year
Children over 12
Wolsey Lodge

The heart of the Lake District is often bustling with visitors so you may prefer to stay with Enid and Hugh Davies in a less commercialized area, make driving forays to the famous beauty spots, and return in the evening to the peace and quiet of Low Hall. Hugh is an anesthetist and Enid was a teacher until she saw Low Hall while house-hunting and decided to put her entertaining skills to work running a guesthouse. Enid says it is like having a house party every night. Guests dine by candlelight in the quaint, beamed dining room (the five-course dinner offers a choice of meat, fish, or vegetarian for the main course) and retire to the comfortable sitting room for coffee, fudge, and a chat. There is plenty of room for the king-sized bed in the flowery Victorian Bedroom. Three other guestrooms, also flowery, are smaller, with snug shower rooms tucked into a corner. I particularly enjoyed the "luxury" bedroom with its attractive decor, television, and attractive bathroom with separate bath and shower. A 3-mile walk along the riverbank brings you to Cockermouth, William Wordsworth's birthplace. Over Whinlatter Pass lies Keswick, a bustling little town at the heart of the Lake District. An hour's drive enables you to visit the forts along Hadrian's Wall. *Directions:* From exit 40 on the M6 take the A66 to Cockermouth and turn left onto the A5086 for 1 mile to the school where you turn left towards Lorton. Low Hall is on your right after 1 mile.

LOW HALL
Owners: Enid & Hugh Davies
Brandlingill
Cockermouth
Cumbria CA13 0RE, England
Tel: (01900) 826654
5 en-suite rooms
From £36 per person dinner, B & B
Open March to November
Children over 10
No-smoking house

Deep in the Devon countryside, in a 16th-century stone-and-cob farmhouse called Lower Beers, Anne Nicholls has realized her dream and founded Bonne Bouche, a residential cooking school. Here she and her husband Gerald provide guests an idyllic spot to perfect their culinary skills. Course offerings include a couple of days designed to remove the angst from entertaining, cooking weeks for keen amateurs, and gourmet tours of the West Country. The Nicholls also welcome guests who are simply on holiday, spending their days exploring the lush Devon countryside and enjoying delicious candlelit dinners in the evenings. The comfortable sitting room offers guests an inviting sofa and chairs in front of the enormous fireplace as well as an assortment of books and magazines. Bedrooms are named after herbs and are fresh and clean, with flower-sprigged bedcovers and matching draperies or wallpapers. Some sightseeing options are to explore Dartmoor and Exmoor and to visit the National Trust properties of Knightshayes and Killerton. *Directions:* Lower Beers is only five minutes from the motorway. Leave the M5 at exit 28 and turn into Cullompton. At the first T-junction turn right towards Willand on the B3181. In 1 mile, just before the pylons, turn left to Brithem Bottom. Lower Beers is the second house on the left after 1 mile.

LOWER BEERS
Owners: Anne & Gerald Nicholls
Brithem Bottom
Cullompton
Devon EX15 1NB, England
Tel: (01884) 32257 Fax: (01884) 32257
3 en-suite rooms
From £27.50 per person
Open all year
Children over 14
No-smoking house
Wolsey Lodge

Gently rolling hills where sheep graze peacefully and shaded valleys with meandering streams surround the picturesque village of Broad Campden where The Malt House hugs the quiet main street. Years ago barley was made into malt here for brewing beer. Now it is a picturesque, very up-market bed and breakfast that provides a perfect central location for exploring other Cotswold villages. A quiet sitting room invites browsing through books and magazines. If requested in advance, dinner or lunch are served on a long table before a massive inglenook fireplace and mullioned windows which offer glimpses of the orchard beyond the garden. All the bedrooms except a small single room face the garden, so guests are ensured a quiet night's repose. The rooms all have plenty of country-cottage charm and several have delightful bathrooms with old-fashioned Victorian tubs. One has a lovely four-poster bed while another is a delightful suite with a sitting room and bedrooms set beneath the eaves up a narrow staircase. Lovely Cotswold villages to explore include Chipping Campden, Bourton-on-the-Water, Upper and Lower Slaughter, Stow-on-the-Wold, Bibury, and Broadway. Garden lovers will enjoy Kiftsgate, Hidcote Manor, and Batsford. *Directions:* On entering Chipping Campden take the first right: you know you are in Broad Campden when you see the Bakers Arms. The Malt House is opposite the wall topped by a tall topiary hedge.

THE MALT HOUSE
Owners: Jean & Nick Brown
Broad Campden
Chipping Campden
Gloucestershire GL55 6UU, England
Tel: (01386) 840295 Fax: (01386) 841334
5 en-suite rooms
From £39.50 per person
Closed Christmas
Children welcome

Just up the lane from The Malt House (our other Broad Campden listing) sits Orchard Hill House, the lovely mellow-stone farmhouse home of Caroline and David Ashmore and their two young children. Their low-beamed dining room sits at the center of the house and it is here that guests gather in the morning to enjoy breakfast round the long refectory-style table before the large inglenook fireplace. Upstairs are two delightfully decorated bedrooms, one with a snug en-suite shower room and the other with its private Victorian-style bathroom across the hall. While the rooms in the main farmhouse are very nice, I really enjoyed the privacy of going up the barn's stone staircase to the lofty, beamed Hayloft. Here you have a spacious room with a sitting area and twin and double beds. An adjacent twin-bedded room is set snugly beneath the barn's low beams. For dinner Caroline directs guests to the Bakers Arms in the village or makes suggestions from amongst the many excellent pubs, restaurants, and bistros in nearby Chipping Campden. Neighboring Snowshill is famous for its toy collection. The beautiful gardens of Kiftsgate and Hidcote are on the way to Stratford-upon-Avon which is just 10 miles away. *Directions:* On entering Chipping Campden take the first right. Pass the Bakers Arms pub and The Malt House, and Orchard Hill House is the next house on your left.

ORCHARD HILL HOUSE
Owners: Caroline & David Ashmore
Broad Campden
Chipping Campden
Gloucestershire GL55 6UU, England
Tel: (01386) 841473 Fax: (01386) 841030
4 rooms, 3 en suite
From £21 per person
Closed Christmas
Children over 2
No-smoking house

Luigi Bellorini came to England many years ago to learn the language. It took him longer than he thought and, while struggling to conjugate his verbs, he fell in love with an English girl, married, and made Britain his home. The desire to cook his national food in his own restaurant lingered and after their children were grown, Luigi and his wife Pauline took the plunge, moved to Broadway, and added an airy conservatory restaurant to this characterful 400-year-old house. Now every evening Luigi can be found in his kitchen creating his culinary magic, while still finding time to visit tables and have a special little chat with each of his patrons. Italian food lovers will be delighted by both the set and à-la-carte menus, though it must be emphasized that the menu is not limited to Italian food nor the wine list to Italian wines. After a delightful dinner and a nightcap in the residents' bar, guests stroll the quiet streets of Broadway before retiring to their rooms up the narrow staircase or across the courtyard. Bedrooms are not fancy but they are prettily decorated and each has its own "teenie" en-suite shower or bathroom. Guests who are staying longer than a couple of nights particularly enjoy the courtyard room with its own private entrance. A stay at Milestone House allows you to enjoy picturesque Broadway in the less crowded hours of early morning and evening. *Directions:* Broadway is on the A44 between Evesham and Stow-on-the-Wold.

MILESTONE HOUSE
Owners: Pauline & Luigi Bellorini
122 High Street
Broadway
Worcestershire WR12 7AJ, England
Tel: (01386) 853432
4 en-suite rooms
From £29.50 per person (no singles)
Closed Christmas
Credit cards: MC, VS
Children welcome

In summer blowzy hollyhocks frame the door of College House, a substantial 17th-century home fronting a quiet street just off the village green of this peaceful Cotswold village. Old flagstones cover the floors, the walls have a soft pastel colorwash, and whimsical stenciling adds decorative interest to the shutters and the old fireplace which displays Sybil's collection of antique bottles. Nothing is cluttered or over-decorated. Sybil used to own a restaurant and is happy with advance notice to provide a three-course dinner. The main bedroom has a huge, luxurious bathroom decked out in blue and white; the bedroom is equally large, with a sleigh bed sitting center stage and an interesting priest hole with a small circular window and stencils of dwarf orange trees in tubs on the walls. Pale-lemon bows decorate the draperies and bed linen of The Yellow Room, blending beautifully with the soft-lemon-colored walls. The slipper tub in the bathroom is perfect for those who enjoy a deep soak and a read. The third bedroom is less expensive because its bathroom is up a spiraling wooden staircase in the attic. While guests visit Bath, Oxford, and Stratford-upon-Avon, Sybil finds what they enjoy most is following her tape that tours them through lesser-known Cotswold villages. *Directions:* From Stow-on-the-Wold take the A429 towards Moreton in Marsh. Turn right at the sign for Broadwell and Evenlode. College House is on your left on the Evenlode side of the village.

COLLEGE HOUSE
Owner: Sybil Gisby
Chapel Street
Broadwell, Moreton in Marsh
Gloucestershire GL56 0TW, England
Tel: (01451) 832351
3 rooms, 2 en suite
From £21 per person
Open all year
Children over 16

The Buck Inn is a traditional Georgian coaching inn standing beneath the towering craggy heights of Buckden Pike which rises steeply behind it. Conviviality and good cheer are the order of the day in the bar where real ale is hand-pulled from the cool stone cellars. In summer there is always a crowd and overnight guests may prefer the quieter restaurant in a bright, enclosed courtyard where in days of old sheep auctions were held. You can enjoy a set four-course dinner with lots of choices for each course or order from the extensive bar menu offering salads, sandwiches, grills, fish, homemade pies, and traditional English fare. Upstairs bedrooms are far more attractive than the mediocre ones on the ground floor. Bedrooms are country-style in their decor, the largest being a four-poster room with a high, raftered ceiling. The surrounding rugged countryside offers many paths for walkers whether they prefer long day hikes or shorter strolls. Wharfedale has several lovely mellow-stone villages such as Grassington, Appletreewick, and Kettlewell. It is a spectacular drive from here through Coverdale to Middleham with its ruined castle and on to Jervaulx with its romantic ruined abbey. To the west, moorland roads lead to Arncliffe and Littondale and on to Malham (in Airedale), famous for its massive crags, tarn, and cove. *Directions:* Buckden is 18 miles north of Skipton on the B6160.

THE BUCK INN
Owners: Marjorie & Roy Hayton
Buckden
Skipton
Yorkshire, BD23 5JA, England
Tel: (01756) 760228 Fax: (01756) 760227
14 en-suite rooms
From £34 per person
Open all year
Credit cards: MC, VS
Children welcome

Set amidst a row of grand Georgian townhouses fronting a broad square, Twelve Angel Hill is a delightful, upscale bed and breakfast operated with great professionalism by Bernadette (Bernie) and John Clarke. Breakfast is the only meal served in the formal dining room where little tables are topped with crisp linen cloths and surrounded by lovely antique chairs. In the evening guests often gather in the bar-cum-sitting room to discuss which of the 40 nearby restaurants or pubs they are going to dine at. Upstairs, the bedrooms range from enormous to snug and all but the four-poster room and the suite are priced the same. I especially enjoyed the two large front bedrooms with spacious seating areas (the four-poster room overlooks the back of the house). Light sleepers be aware there may be a little late-night noise from the square on Fridays and Saturdays. On the square you have the 16th-century cathedral and the church of St. Mary's (even older than the cathedral), and nearby two museums. If you are there on a Wednesday or Saturday, do not miss the street market. Lavenham and Cambridge are popular places to visit. *Directions:* Follow the A14 to the Bury St. Edmunds ring road. Take the second exit (Bury St. Edmunds central) then at the next roundabout turn into Northgate Street. At the T-junction turn right into the square and Twelve Angel Hill is on your right—parking is to the rear. If arriving by train, take a taxi from the station.

TWELVE ANGEL HILL   **NEW**
Owners: Bernadette (Bernie) & John Clarke
12 Angel Hill
Bury St. Edmunds
Suffolk IP33 1UZ, England
Tel: (01284) 704088 Fax: (01284) 725549
6 en-suite rooms
From £32.50 per person
Closed January
Credit cards: all major
Children over 16
No-smoking house

Butlers is a 17th-century farmhouse sitting in secluded countryside, ideally located for touring the pretty villages and churches of Suffolk and Essex. Butlers' exterior is covered with traditional pargettry (ornamental plasterwork) while the inside is all beams and cottagey rooms. Guests enjoy a comfortable sitting room with a piano and a small television. Sylvia is happy to provide a dinner that can range from a simple supper to a more elaborate, three-course meal or she helps guests choose from several restaurants and pubs within a 10-mile radius. Upstairs, the bedrooms come in three sizes. A snug double and twin-bedded room share a bathroom. A larger, beamed room has an en-suite bathroom. The biggest, an L-shaped double room, enjoys a large bed and an en-suite bathroom with the bathtub, loo, and washbasin tucked into an alcove beside the bed. Colchester, the oldest recorded town in England (with its museum, libraries, and art galleries) is 9 miles away. Sudbury (6 miles) offers Gainsborough's birthplace and museum, while Constable's Flatford Mill lies across the valley. Antique shops abound in Long Melford, Clare, and Lavenham. *Directions:* Bures is on the B1508 between Colchester and Sudbury. From Sudbury cross the river into Bures Hamlet. Bear right on the left hand bend, under the railway bridge, and turn immediately left into Colne Road. Butlers is on your left after 1 mile.

BUTLERS
Owners: Sylvia & Paul Roberts
Colne Road
Bures Hamlet
Bures
Suffolk CO8 5DN, England
Tel: (01787) 227243
3 rooms, 2 en suite
From £19 per person
Closed Christmas
Children over 5

The clomp of hooves as horses pulled carriages down the main street of Burford has long disappeared, but the inns that provided lodging and food to weary travelers remain and if you are in search of a simple, quaint hostelry, you can do no better than to base yourself at The Lamb for the duration of your stay in the Cotswolds. A tall, upholstered settle sits before the fireplace on the flagstone floor of the main room, the hall table displays gleaming brass jelly molds, and an air of times long past pervades the place, particularly in winter when the air is heavy with the scent of woodsmoke and a flickering fire burns in the grate. Narrow staircases and corridors zigzag up and down to the little bedrooms, all simply decorated in a charming cottagey style. In the dining room the four-course dinner menu, with lots of choices for each course, is priced according to what is selected for the main course. The homely little bar with its stone-flagged floor and wooden settles has an indefinable mixture of character and atmosphere. Burford's main street is bordered by numerous antique, gift, and tea shops. There are mellow-stone Cotswold villages to explore and Blenheim Palace and Oxford are less than an hour's drive away. *Directions:* Burford is midway between Oxford and Cheltenham (A40). The Lamb Inn is on Sheep Street, just off the village center.

THE LAMB INN
Owners: Caroline & Richard De Wolf
Sheep Street
Burford
Oxfordshire OX18 4LR, England
Tel: (01993) 823155
16 rooms, 14 en suite
From £42.50 per person
Closed Christmas
Credit cards: MC, VS
Children welcome

Built over a century ago, Chilvester Hill House is a solidly constructed Victorian home isolated from the busy A4 by a large garden. Gill and John Dilley retired here and subsequently unretired themselves: John, a physician, now works as an occupational health consultant and Gill entertains guests and breeds beef cattle. Gill enjoys cooking and a typical (optional) dinner might consist of smoked trout, lamb noisettes with vegetables from the garden, fruit fool, and cheese and biscuits. They have a short wine list with over 20 French and German wines. A soft pastel decor, treasured antiques, and a cleverly displayed collection of commemorative plates make the large, high-ceilinged drawing room the most elegant room in the house. The bedrooms are spacious, high-ceilinged rooms, each individually decorated with flowery Sanderson wallpaper (two have zip-link beds that can be either a king or twins). All have mineral water, tea and coffee tray, television, tourist information, and private bathroom. Visitors can enjoy the heated swimming pool during the summer months or take advantage of Gill and John's mimeographed maps marked with scenic routes to nearby Castle Combe, Lacock, and the Avebury Neolithic Circle. Bath, Oxford, and Salisbury are an easy drive away. *Directions:* From London leave the M4 at junction 14 and follow signs for Hungerford. Turn right on the A4 through Marlborough to Calne. Follow Chippenham signs for half a mile, turn right (Bremhill), and immediately right into the drive.

CHILVESTER HILL HOUSE
Owners: Gill & John Dilley
Calne
Wiltshire SN11 0LP, England
Tel: (01249) 813981 Fax: (01249) 814217
3 en-suite rooms
From £30 per person
Open all year
Credit cards: all major
Children over 12
Wolsey Lodge

A county lane winds through Coverdale, one of the quieter Yorkshire dales, and leads to the few cottages and traditional dales pub, the Foresters Arms, that make up the village of Carlton. You enter into the snug low-ceilinged bar where you can enjoy ale on tap with the locals and warm yourself by the fire on cool evenings. The food is far more sophisticated than the run-of-the-mill pub grub and can be enjoyed in the bar or the little restaurant. Up the narrow stone staircase you find three small cottagey bedrooms and a quiet sitting area. Room 2 offers the most spacious accommodation (double bed) while room 1 (a twin) has a lovely view of the dale. Both have snug en-suite shower rooms. Room 3, a twin, has its private bathroom across the hall. Coverdale is a quieter, smaller dale that connects the busier Wharfedale to Wensleydale. Your hosts Julie Harrington and Barry Higginbottom are happy to assist in planning walking and driving tours that encompass the stunning Yorkshire dales scenery and the characterful market towns. The ancient castles at Bolton, Skipton, and Middleham and the old abbeys of Jervaulx, Fountains, and Bolton are also worth a visit. *Directions:* Leave the A1 on the A6108 to Masham and on to Middleham. Proceed straight through the market square past the ruins of Middleham castle and into Coverdale. A 3-mile drive brings you to Carlton.

FORESTERS ARMS   **NEW**
Owners: Julie Harrington & Barry Higginbottom
Carlton
Near Leyburn
Yorkshire DL8 2BB, England
Tel & fax: (01969) 640272
3 rooms, 2 en suite
From £30 per person
Open all year
Credit cards: MC, VS
Children welcome

Because of its quiet country location just 3 miles off the motorway, almost equidistant between Edinburgh and London, New Capernwray Farm is an ideal place to break a long, tiring journey. However, many weary travelers return for a proper country getaway to explore this unspoiled area. There really is nothing "new" about this solid, whitewashed stone farmhouse, for despite its name, it is approaching its 300th birthday. It was bought in 1974 by Sally and Peter Townend, who supervised its complete refurbishment while preserving its lovely old features, and now offer a very warm welcome to their guests. Before dinner you enjoy sherry in the cozy sitting room in front of a cheerful fire and then proceed to the dining room for a candlelit dinner. Bedrooms are particularly light, bright, and cheerful in their decor. The largest bedroom spans the breadth of the house, has a bathroom tucked neatly under the eaves and, as in all the rooms, is well equipped with tea, coffee, biscuits, television, hairdryer, mints, and a substantial sewing kit. A twin-bedded room has an en-suite shower room and the double-bedded room has its shower room nearby. Sally and Peter offer guided tours and have a wealth of books and maps on the Lake District and the Yorkshire dales. *Directions:* Leave the M6 at junction 35 and from the roundabout follow signs for Over Kellet. Turn left at the T-junction into Over Kellet, then turn left at the village green: after 2 miles the farm is on the left.

NEW CAPERNWRAY FARM
Owners: Sally & Peter Townend
Capernwray
Carnforth
Lancashire LA6 1AD, England
Tel & fax: (01524) 734284
3 rooms, 2 en suite
From £28.50 per person
Open all year
Children over 10
Wolsey Lodge

Thruxted Oast, conveniently located about a 10-minute drive south of Canterbury, like so many fine old buildings, was in a most dilapidated condition before being rescued by Hilary and Tim Derouet and transformed into a lovely home. The ground floor has a dining room and a parlor, but the heart of the house is the family-style kitchen where guests gather each morning at a large antique farmhouse table for a delicious breakfast. Upstairs the three guest bedrooms are cleverly converted from the three original drying stalls with their high-peaked wooden ceilings and massive rafters. These spacious, twin-bedded rooms are attractively papered with a tiny print design which is complemented by pretty, short drapes at the windows. The same pattern is repeated in the handmade patchwork quilts, throw pillows, and dressing table skirts: my favorite room, Chaucer, features soft pink and green tones. Tim used to be a farmer and evidence of his green thumb can be seen in the lovely garden stretching behind the oast where abundant flowers border a verdant green lawn. Canterbury is 4 miles away. *Directions:* From Canterbury take the A28 towards Ashford. On the city outskirts cross the A2 and after 200 yards turn left on St. Nicholas Road. At the end T-junction, turn right and continue 2 miles, past St. Augustine Hospital. Continue straight over the cross road and down the hill to Thruxted Oast on the right.

THRUXTED OAST
Owners: Hilary & Tim Derouet
Chartham
Canterbury
Kent CT4 7BX, England
Tel: (01227) 730080
3 en-suite rooms
From £37.50 per person
Closed Christmas
Credit cards: all major
Children over 12

Theresa White, who hails from Edinburgh, prides herself on offering a warm Scottish welcome to her up-market bed-and-breakfast hotel located a brisk 20-minute walk from the heart of medieval Chester. When she bought Redland in the 1980s it was very different from the flower-decked, frothily Victorian establishment you find today. Theresa has kept all the lovely woodwork and ornate plasterwork, adding modern bathrooms, central heating, vast quantities of sturdy Victorian furniture, four suits of armor, and masses of Victorian bric-a-brac. Guests help themselves to drinks at the honesty bar and relax in the sumptuous drawing room which includes among its array of furniture high-backed armchairs which almost surround you. Traditional Scottish porridge is a must when you order breakfast in the dining room where little tables are covered with starched Victorian tablecloths. For dinner Theresa is happy to advise on where to eat in town. Pay the few extra pounds and request one of the "best" rooms, for not only are they more spacious, but you will be treated to a lovely old bed (with modern mattress, of course) and decor where everything from the draperies to the china is color-coordinated. Walking round Chester's Roman walls is a good way to orient yourself to the city. It is fun to browse in The Rows, double-decker layers of shops. *Directions:* Redland Hotel is located on the A5104 1 mile from the city center.

REDLAND HOTEL
Owner: Theresa White
64 Hough Green
Chester CH4 8JY, England
Tel: (01244) 671024 Fax: (01244) 681309
12 en-suite rooms
From £30 per person
Open all year
Children over 2

Chiddingfold, with its attractive homes set round the village green, is one of the most picturesque villages on the wooded Surrey Downs. A dovecote fronts the country lane just off the village green and a path leads beside it through a picture-book English cottage garden to Greenaway, the charming home of Sheila and John Marsh. The interior is just as delightful as the exterior, with low-ceilinged, beamed rooms, each decorated to perfection without making them stiffly formal or contrived. Guests enjoy the lovely living room with its views of the garden and part of Sheila and John's collection of colorful Staffordshire pottery displayed on the mantelshelf above the massive fireplace. Breakfast is served in the cozy dining room or, if guests prefer to sit and chat, they can eat their breakfast at the trestle table in the kitchen. For dinner guests often walk down to the 12th-century Crown hotel in the village. The large front bedroom enjoys a new, old-fashioned bathroom with a claw-foot tub. The spacious blue twin and a third bedroom share a large immaculate bathroom. Chiddingfold is conveniently located 40 miles from both Gatwick and Heathrow airports. Guests often visit Petworth house, Bignor Roman villa, Chichester, Portsmouth, and the south coast. *Directions:* From Guildford take the A3 and the A283 to Chiddingfold. Pickhurst Road is off the green and Greenaway is the third house on the left with the large dovecote in front.

GREENAWAY
Owners: Sheila & John Marsh
Pickhurst Road
Chiddingfold
Surrey GU8 4TS, England
Tel: (01428) 682920 Fax: (01428) 685078
3 rooms, 1 en suite
From £27.50 per person
Closed Christmas
Children welcome

Ashen Clough, Isobel and Norman Salisbury's home, began life in the 16th century as a prosperous yeoman's home set in a rural Derbyshire valley. Norman was for many years the local vet then retired to take on domestic duties, helping Isobel run their lovely home as the most welcoming of Wolsey Lodges. Guests dine with their hosts around the ancient refectory table in the low-beamed dining room. Drinks in the comfortable drawing room precede dinner and it is here that guests enjoy coffee and evening-long conversation before retiring to their delightful bedrooms. On Sunday evenings, Isobel and Norman excuse themselves as host and hostess and a sumptuous buffet is provided. Country lanes lead to main roads that quickly transport you to Georgian Buxton with its restored opera house, Bakewell with its shops and Monday market, the Potteries where you can visit the Royal Crown Derby factories and factory shops, and the great houses of Chatsworth, Haddon, Keddleston, and Lyme Hall. *Directions:* From Buxton take the A6 (Manchester road) for 6 miles and at the roundabout turn left at the signpost for Chinley. Follow the B6062 into the village where you turn right and then right again into Maynestone Road. Ashen Clough is on your left after 1¼ miles.

ASHEN CLOUGH
Owners: Isobel & Norman Salisbury
Maynestone Road
Chinley
Derbyshire SK12 6AH, England
Tel: (01663) 750311
3 rooms, 2 en suite
From £28.50 person
Open all year
Children over 16
Wolsey Lodge

If you want to stay in a 600-year-old cottage at the heart of an idylically pretty Cotswold town, you can do no better than Rosary Cottage, Rosemary Spencer's home in the center of Chipping Campden's High Street. However, be aware that this is one of the most popular Cotswold towns and parking in the daytime can be problematic. In the evening the tourists depart and the cottage-lined streets are yours to enjoy. Inside, Rosary Cottage is all exposed beams, low doorways, and sloping floors. Up the narrow stairs, the snug bedrooms are beautifully decorated and each has either a tiny en-suite shower room or its bathroom just outside the door—all are quite unsuitable for large suitcases. Rosemary encourages friendly conversation round the breakfast table and provides her guests with a bountiful repast—she used to be the breakfast cook at the Lords of the Manor hotel. Chipping Campden has an ancient market hall where sheep from the surrounding farms were sold, and there are lots of interesting little shops, two old churches, and a wide variety of restaurants, bistros, and pubs. A short distance away lies Hidcote, a series of alluring gardens each bordered by sculptured hedges and linked with paths and terraces. Next door, Kiftsgate has exquisite displays of roses. *Directions:* From Broadway take the A44, towards Stow on the Wold, up the hill and turn left for Chipping Campden. At the T-junction turn right into High Street and Rosary Cottage is on your left midway down the road.

ROSARY COTTAGE
Owner: Rosemary Spencer
Chipping Campden
Gloucestershire GL55 6AL, England
Tel: (01386) 841145
3 rooms, 2 en suite
From £22 per person
Open all year
Children over 3

Oakfield is the elegant, early-Victorian home of Patricia and Peter Johnson King, a home where standards surpass those of many country house hotels. Decorated in soft pinks and blue-grays, the enormous drawing room is warm and welcoming on even the dullest of days, its tall windows overlooking a broad sweep of lawns. Past the grand piano and up the elegant staircase are three lovely bedrooms. Elizabeth's Room has a half-tester bed softly draped in pale cream and turquoise with a huge claw-foot tub in the bathroom; Rose is a mass of pink and soft-blue cabbage roses; and Chinese is smartly Oriental with peach watered-silk wallpaper and a black satin bedspread coordinating with peach-and-black draperies. With advance notice, Patricia is happy to cook a four-course dinner where she and Peter dine with their guests. Otherwise, guests often walk to Highwayman's Haunt in the village. A full-size billiard room is there for you to use as is a large heated swimming pool. The gardens contain an unusual Victorian fern garden. Oakfield is ideally situated for exploring Dartmoor National Park, the cathedral city of Exeter, and the south Devon coast. *Directions:* From Exeter take the A38 towards Plymouth for 8 miles. Turn left for Chudleigh and after 1 mile Oakfield is on your right before you come to the center of the village.

OAKFIELD
Owners: Patricia & Peter Johnson King
Chudleigh
Devon TQ13 0DD, England
Tel: (01626) 852194 Fax: (01626) 852194
3 en-suite rooms
From £30 per person
Open March to October
Children over 12
Wolsey Lodge

This pretty village of flint-walled, tile-roofed cottages is no longer "next the sea," but separated from it by a vast saltwater marsh formed as the sea retreated. The massive structure of Cley Mill stands as a handsome monument to man's ability to harness the forces of nature. Guests enter the mill directly into the beamed dining room decorated with country-style pine furniture. The circular sitting room has large chintz chairs drawn round a stone fireplace whose mantel is a sturdy beam displaying toby jugs. Stacked above the sitting room are two large circular bedrooms with en-suite bathrooms: the Wheat Chamber is where the grain was stored and the Stone Room is where the massive grinding stones crushed the flour. Two additional small bedrooms share a bathroom. During the day the mill is open to the public to visit the observation room and the wooden cap of the mill with its massive gears and complex mechanisms which once turned the grinding stones. The old boat house and stables in the yard have been converted into small, self-catering cottages. Birdwatching, sailing, cycling, and walking are popular pastimes in the area. The seaside towns of Sheringham, Cromer, and Wells are close at hand. There are a great many stately homes to explore such as Sandringham House, the Royal Family's country residence, Jacobean Fellbrigg Hall, Holkham, and Blickling Hall. *Directions:* From King's Lynn follow the A149 around the coast to Cley next the Sea, where the windmill is well signposted.

CLEY MILL GUEST HOUSE
Managers: Jenny & Tim Mallam
Cley next the Sea
Holt
Norfolk NR25 7NN, England
Tel: (01263) 740209 Fax: (01263) 740209
7 rooms, 5 en suite
From £31.50 per person
Closed February
Children over 6

Sun Hill, a Yorkshire Dales farmhouse, is the loveliest of places to stay: a home that is furnished with enviable antiques, decorated in great style, and where Angela and Ian Close offer guests the warmest of hospitality and lovely food. The flagstone hallway leads to the conservatory where guests gather for pre-dinner drinks (drinks and wine are included in the tariff). Angela and Ian dine with their guests and join them afterwards in the sunny yellow sitting room with its comfortable Victorian chairs for coffee and conversation which often continues late into the night. Upstairs, the snug double bedroom has a spacious modern bathroom where Angela has painted a lovely frieze of wildflowers on the bathroom tile. The equally lovely twin-bedded room offers more space and has its large en-suite bathroom down a few stairs. Angela is an expert on antique shops and showrooms in the area—she has a good selection of bric-a-brac for sale in the adjacent barn and a stall at a local Sunday antique market. Sun Hill is ideally located for exploring the Yorkshire Dales, North York Moors, York, Castle Howard, and Fountains Abbey. Small wonder that guests return again and again. *Directions:* Exit the A1 at Bedale and turn right through the town towards Leyburn. Go through Crake Hall and Patrick Brompton to Constable Burton. Cross the bridge and turn first left. Follow the lane for 1 mile and Sun Hill is on your right near the top of the hill.

SUN HILL   **NEW**
Owners: Angela & Ian Close
Constable Burton, Leyburn
North Yorkshire DL8 5RL, England
Tel: (01677) 450303
2 en-suite rooms
From £50 per person, dinner, bed & breakfast
Open all year
Children welcome

Judy and Mike Ford confess to loving sailing, gardening, and Treviades Barton, their Cornish farmhouse. While parts of the house date back to the 13th century, much of what you see today is the result of an extensive modernization in 1580. The ancient uneven flagstone floor leads you from the kitchen to the spacious low-ceilinged living room overlooking the walled garden. Follow the garden path from one flower-filled garden to another—this is where camellias bloom from January to June. With advance notice, Judy is happy to prepare dinner, which includes wine, and she and Mike usually join their guests. One of the bedrooms has an en-suite bathroom and little sitting area around the back of the chimney. If you are traveling with children, request the former children's rooms where two bedrooms share a bathroom. If you would like to see the hidden villages and gardens of Cornwall without all the hassles of navigating your car down very narrow lanes, the Fords can put you in contact with James Agnew who specializes in personalized tours of this part of the country. *Directions:* From Truro take the A39 towards Falmouth. A small white sign indicates the turnoff to Constantine from the Hillhead roundabout on the A39 as it bypasses Penryn. Follow the signs for Constantine. Half a mile after High Cross garage turn left towards Port Navas and Treviades Barton is on your left (no name on the house).

TREVIADES BARTON   **NEW**
Owners: Judy & Mike Ford
High Cross
Constantine, near Falmouth
Cornwall TR11 5RG, England
Tel & fax: (01326) 340524
3 rooms, 2 en suite
From £18 per person
Closed Christmas
Credit cards: MC, VS
Children welcome

Just steps from the clifftops on an isolated stretch of Cornish coast, this 16th-century farmhouse snuggles in a hollow round a cobbled courtyard. The polished flagstone floors lead you into the comfortable sitting room with high-backed sofas grouped round the log-burning stove. Guests dine at separate tables and Janet Crocker offers a hearty dinner with a choice of starter, main course, and dessert. Farmhouse bedrooms range from small to spacious. If you are a party of four, opt for the roomier contemporary accommodation offered by nearby Samphire House. Here you enjoy two double bedrooms and a large sitting room with a balcony which overlooks a sheltered swimming pool. It's very much a family operation where Janet runs the farmhouse while her husband, four sons and their wives manage the farm, tea room, and self-catering cottages. A visitors' center emphasizes the preservation of this lovely coastline. The clifftops offer magnificent views and a path leads to Strangles Beach where Thomas Hardy loved to walk with his first wife Emma. Walking the coastal path and the nearby villages of Boscastle and Tintagel are great attractions. *Directions:* From Bude, take the A39 towards Camelford and then turn right to Crackington Haven. At the beach, take the right-hand turn at the bottom of the hill for Trevigue and you find Trevigue Farm atop the cliffs after 2 miles.

TREVIGUE FARM
Owners: Janet & Ken Crocker & family
Crackington Haven
Bude
Cornwall EX23 0LQ, England
Tel & fax: (01840) 230418
5 en-suite rooms
From £20 per person
Open March to October
Children over 12

This picture-book farmhouse surrounded by a pretty garden and apple orchards is idyllic and just a two-minute drive from the attractive town of Cranbrook with its white-board houses and shops, medieval church, and huge, white-board windmill with vast sails. Guests have a large sitting/dining room with comfy chairs set before an enormous inglenook fireplace and a dining table for breakfast and dinner. The large downstairs bedroom has views to the garden and an en-suite shower room, and is large enough to accommodate an extra bed. Up a broad flight of creaking stairs is a glorious four-poster room where sunny yellow fabrics complement the dark woods of the floor and bed. The third bedroom has a small sitting room and en-suite bathroom and is prettily decorated with Laura Ashley fabrics. Sissinghurst Castle with its lovely garden is nearby and Bridget and Robin find that guests often visit Canterbury and its famous cathedral—they encourage them to time their visit to include choral evensong. The local vineyards and old railway at Tenterden are other popular attractions. *Directions:* Take the A21 south from Sevenoaks, turn left at the A262 before Lamberhurst, and right onto the A229. Go into Cranbrook and take a sharp left after the school. Tilsden Lane (not marked) is the third right, and Hancocks' driveway is the first track on the left.

HANCOCKS FARMHOUSE
Owners: Bridget & Robin Oaten
Tilsden Lane
Cranbrook
Kent TN17 3PH, England
Tel: (01580) 714645
3 en-suite rooms
From £25 per person
Closed Christmas
Children over 9

Everything about The Old Cloth Hall is exceptional, from the vast expanses of gardens with manicured lawns, roses, rhododendrons, and azaleas to the dignified old house, parts of which date back more than 500 years. Settle into the richly paneled drawing room with its commodious sofas and chairs drawn round the crackling log fire which blazes in the enormous inglenook. The Old Cloth Hall has been Katherine Morgan's home for many years and because it is a large house she has an array of bedrooms that can be used for guest accommodation which she prices by size and location. If you are on a stringent budget, request the small downstairs twin. If you want to splurge, ask for The Four Poster room and you will receive a king-size four-poster decked and draped in lemon-and-green-sprigged fabric with an enormous bathroom. Elizabeth I came for lunch in 1573 but you can stay for dinner and dine with your fellow guests. Guests are welcome to use the unheated swimming pool and the tennis court. Cranbrook is one hour from London, Dover, Canterbury, and Brighton. Sir Winston Churchill's home, Chartwell, Knole, Igtham Mote, Penshurt Place, and Batemans, Rudyard Kipling's home, are within easy reach. *Directions:* Take the A21 south from Sevenoaks, turn left at the A262 before Lamberhurst and right onto the A229 towards Tenterden. Go into Cranbrook and take a sharp left after the school, follow this road for about a mile, turn right just before the cemetery, and the entrance to The Old Cloth Hall is on your right.

THE OLD CLOTH HALL
Owner: Katherine Morgan
Cranbrook
Kent TN17 3NR, England
Tel: (01580) 712220
3 en-suite rooms
From £37.50 per person
Open all year
Children by arrangement
Wolsey Lodge

When you stay at The Old Manor, you get far more than bed-and-breakfast in a 16th-century house—you can tour its motor museum, make friends with the army of ducks and geese that wander around the yard, and visit the contented, muddy pigs who wallow at the bottom of the garden. Inside there are cozy beamed rooms and the gentle ticking of Liz and John's clock collection. Books line the walls of the breakfast room and guests eat together round the trestle table before a log fire. The small yellow sitting room at the top of the stairs is for guests to use. A large double bedroom has a snug, en-suite shower room while the two twin rooms share a bathroom down the hallway. Liz is very aware that guests always enjoy their own bathroom facilities, so she rents only one of the twin bedrooms at a time. John is happy to show you his transportation collection which includes an AC Cobra, a 1910 AC Sociable, and a 1934 Aston Martin. If you are planning on staying for a week, consider renting the delightful little Dovehouse Barn. Warwick Castle, Coventry, and a multitude of Cotswold villages are within half an hour's drive. The Oxford Canal runs along the bottom of the garden and you can walk for miles along its towpath. *Directions:* Exit the M40 at junction 11 (Banbury) and take the A361 towards Daventry for 2½ miles, turn left to Cropredy, cross the canal, turn left at the T-junction, and The Old Manor is on your left.

THE OLD MANOR
Owners: Liz & John Atkins
Cropredy, Banbury
Oxfordshire OX17 1PS, England
Tel: (01295) 750235 Fax: (01295) 758479
3 rooms, 1 en suite
From £22 per person
Closed Christmas & New Year
Credit cards: all major
Children welcome
No-smoking house

Fulford House is one of those interesting homes that has evolved over the years. The earliest parts date back to the 1600s with various bits added from time to time—hence the interesting way you step up and down as you go from room to room. Guests are welcomed as visiting friends and encouraged to make themselves at home in the comfortable sitting room with its slipcovered chairs and soft-peach walls. Blowzy roses decorate the curtains and bed ruffles of the largest bedroom whose en-suite bathroom is up a short flight of stairs. A large twin room and a small single sharing a bathroom across the hall are suitable for families. A booklet in each bedroom gives an in-depth history of Culworth and suggests enough sightseeing excursions to keep you busy for a week, including Sulgrave Manor, George Washington's ancestral home, Warwick Castle, Stratford-upon-Avon, Coventry cathedral, exquisite Hidcote Manor gardens, and Fulford House's own acre of delightful gardens which Marypen and Stephen are justifiably very proud of. *Directions:* From the M40 junction 11 roundabout take the A422 towards Brackley, then after 1 mile take B4525 signposted Northampton. After 2 miles turn left to Culworth. Turn right alongside the village green and Fulford House is on your left.

FULFORD HOUSE
Owners: Marypen & Stephen Wills
Culworth
Banbury
Oxfordshire OX17 2BB, England
Tel: (01295) 760355 Fax: (01295) 768304
3 rooms, 1 en suite
From £24 per person
Open mid-February to mid-November
Children over 5

With its medieval beamed barn, creeper-covered farmhouse, and flower-filled courtyard, Hillards presents an inviting picture. Owners Jeannie Wilkins and Mike Carter and their four cats welcome guests to their farmhouse where they enjoy both a television room and a comfortable lounge for relaxing. The rooms tend to be on the dark side: dark wooden furniture, dark fabrics, small windows, dark oak paneling, and exposed, gray stone walls do not give a light and airy feel to the house. While I enjoyed the Jacuzzi tub in the master bedroom, the courtyard room with its little window seats was a special favorite. Breakfast is the only meal served, though plans are under way to convert the ancient barn into a restaurant. Strung out along a busy road, Curry Rivel village is not a tourist destination but Jeannie will outline a driving tour that quickly has you deep in pretty countryside visiting her favorite willow basket producers. Wells with its gorgeous cathedral and Glastonbury steeped in Arthurian legend are popular places to visit. *Directions:* Leave the M25 motorway at junction 25, taking the A358 towards Chard to the A378 to Curry Rivel. Hillards is on your left as you enter the village.

HILLARDS
Owners: Jeannie Wilkins & Mike Carter
High Street
Curry Rivel
Langport
Somerset TA10 0EY, England
Tel: (01458) 251737 Fax: (01458) 253233
3 en-suite rooms
From £27.50 per person
Open all year
Children over 12

The Cott Inn is the longest thatched building in Devon and certainly one of the prettiest pubs in England with its little windows peeking out coyly from beneath the thatch and the garden a blaze of color. On entering, you see a comfortable bar with low, beamed ceiling, horse brasses, log fire, and locals drinking pints of bitter. A wide selection of dinner specials is posted on the blackboard or you can choose from the short steak menu. If you prefer to eat in more sophisticated surroundings, choose the little dining room where a tempting array of desserts is laid out on the buffet. Up the narrow winding staircases the cozy bedrooms tucked under the thatch come in attractive doubles or twins and are accompanied by en-suite bathrooms or shower rooms. Just down the road is Dartington's Cider Press shopping center where in amongst the craft shops you find the Dartington Glass Shop. Nearby Totnes has its castle and streets of ancient buildings: on Tuesdays in summer the townsfolk dress in Elizabethan costume. Farther afield lie Elizabethan Dartmouth with its naval college, picturesque Salcombe, Buckfastleigh with its abbey, and the wild expanses of Dartmoor National Park. *Directions:* Travel on the A38 towards Plymouth when the M5 ends and turn left on the A384 towards Totnes. As you enter Dartington, pass a church on your left and at the next roundabout take the second exit to Cott. Cott Inn is on your right after half a mile

COTT INN   **NEW**
Owners: Susan & David Grey
Cott, Dartington
Devon TQ9 6HE, England
Tel: (01803) 863777 Fax: (01803) 866629
6 en-suite rooms
From £25 per person
Open all year
Credit cards: all major
Children over 5

Ford House is a three-story, Regency-style home which was built for the owner of one of the many shipyards that flourished in Dartmouth during the 19th century. Australian owner Dick Turner's easy, laid-back manner is echoed in his partner Henri (Henrietta) Firth. Guests go upstairs and downstairs to their bedrooms from the combination sitting and dining room. Garden-level bedrooms are confusingly called the King Room (it has an American queen-sized bed) and the Twin Room, which, more often than not, has its twin beds zipped together as a king. Upstairs you find Tony's Room, where old sewing machines decorate the top of the armoire and the bed is placed at an angle to capture the view across the rooftops of the town. While there are lots of restaurants in town, Henri is happy, with advance notice, to provide an evening meal if guests do not want to go out again after a long day's sightseeing. A fun day trip involves taking a ferry and steam train into Paignton. On Tuesdays, in summer, you can take the ferry to Totnes and stroll around the market admiring the townsfolk in their colorful Elizabethan costumes. *Directions:* From Totnes, take the A381 to Halwell and the A3122 to Dartmouth, where you take the first feeder lane to the right into Townstal Road, which becomes Victoria Road. If you go down a long straight hill, you've gone too far.

FORD HOUSE
Owners: Henrietta Firth & Dick Turner
44 Victoria Road
Dartmouth
Devon TQ6 9DX, England
Tel & fax: (01803) 834047
3 en-suite rooms
From £32.50 per person
Open March to December
Credit cards: MC, VS
Children welcome

Hunts Tor offers the opportunity not only for very comfortable bed and breakfast accommodation but also for enjoying excellent food (Paul Henderson of Gidleigh Park assured me that, next to Gidleigh Park, Sue Harrison offers the finest food on Dartmoor). Every evening Sue prepares a set, four-course dinner and while she is busy in the kitchen husband Chris helps guests choose wine and serves at table. Fortunately for diners, the Harrisons also offer the highest quality accommodation (Gidleigh Park excluded, of course!) in the area. Three very spacious bedrooms are large enough to accommodate seating areas, while the fourth room is a snug double-bedded room. A feature of the village is the thatched Drewe Arms, a characterful pub which has changed not a jot since 1919 when Mabel Mudge became landlady. Since Mabel's retirement in 1995 the brewery and the village have been in debate over what to do with this historic landmark. The raw beauty of Dartmoor with its sheltered villages and market towns, wild ponies, and spectacular scenery is a magnet for walkers and those touring by car. Just beyond the village you find Castle Drogo, the castle-like house designed by Lutyens. *Directions:* Take the M5 to Exeter and the A30 towards Oakhampton for about 14 miles. Turn left for Drewsteignton (3 miles) and upon reaching the village square turn right. Hunts Tor is at the opposite end of the square from the church.

HUNTS TOR **NEW**
Owners: Sue & Chris Harrison
Drewsteignton
Devon EX6 6QW, England
Tel: (01647) 281228
4 en-suite rooms
From £22 per person
Open March to October
Children over 10

Dunster, with its adorable main street dominated by the battlements and towers of Dunster Castle, is a picture-postcard village. Dollons House, once a pharmacy whose chemist also made marmalade for the Houses of Parliament, is a gift shop of English crafts and silk flowers where proprietor Humphrey Bradshaw makes his marmalade for his family and bed and breakfast guests. Up the narrow cottage stairs guests have a cozy sitting room that leads to a patio and pocket-sized garden. Hannah Bradshaw has taken a great deal of care decorating her very pretty bedrooms. Teddy, as the name implies, has cute bears embroidered on its towels and pillows and a whimsical honey-bear mural decorating the tiny shower room. Tulips is soft and country in pale pinks with hand-painted tulips on the fabric border which edges the room. Kate's at the back of the house is delightfully white and frilly with a large bathroom and shower. Dunster Castle is open to the public and you can tour the 18th-century Dunster watermill. *Directions:* From Bridgwater take the A39 almost to Minehead. Turn left on the A396 into Dunster, and Dollons is in Church Street on your right. Pull up outside to unload then park in the High Street or behind the church.

DOLLONS HOUSE
Owners: Hannah & Humphrey Bradshaw
Church Street
Dunster
Minehead
Somerset TA24 6SH, England
Tel: (01643) 821880
3 en-suite rooms
From £23.50 per person
Closed Christmas & Boxing Day
Credit cards: MC, VS
Children over 15
No-smoking house

Drakestone House is an exceptional Cotswold-style home filled with an abundance of lovely antiques. The well kept grounds invite a leisurely stroll between the tall, clipped hedges laid out by Hugh's grandfather. The interior of Drakestone House has lovely old pine-pitch-and-jarrah wood floors and beamed-and-plasterwork ceilings, complemented by traditional firebaskets filled with dried flower arrangements and beautiful old furniture. Guests enjoy breakfast round the dining room table where Crystal will, with advance arrangements, also serve dinner for guests' first evening's stay. Upstairs, two bedrooms share the facilities of an old-fashioned bathroom which has been modernized. There is also a suite which has an adjoining private bath, a small twin-bedded room suitable for children (crib available), and a larger, double-bedded room which has windows with views both to the side and the front of the house. From Drakestone House you can visit Berkeley Castle and the adjacent Jenner Museum, Slimbridge Wildfowl Trust, Westonbirt Arboretum, and, farther afield, Gloucester, Cheltenham, Bath, and Bristol. *Directions:* Northbound travelers leave the M5 at exit 14; southbound at exit 13. Stinchcombe is situated halfway between Dursley and Wotton-under-Edge on the B4060. Drakestone House is signposted on the road.

DRAKESTONE HOUSE
Owners: Crystal & Hugh St. John Mildmay
Stinchcombe
Dursley
Gloucestershire GL11 6AS, England
Tel: (01453) 542140
3 rooms, none en suite
From £25 per person
Open April to October
Children welcome
No-smoking house
Wolsey Lodge

Ronald is the keenest of gardeners and his acres of grounds are a delight: plant-filled borders line the tumbling stream, the herbaceous border is ablaze with summer flowers, and the water meadow offers some unusual plant species. Jackie loves to share her beautiful home with guests who can choose from three very different bedrooms. The Cottage Suite offers a low-ceilinged bedroom, snug sitting room with television and VCR with sofas which can be made into extra beds, and a small bathroom. In contrast, the Master Suite offers a large high-ceilinged room with a queen-sized bed, television and VCR, and a large, luxurious Victorian-style bathroom. The Pine Bedroom takes its name from the enormous pine fitted cupboard that has been there since the house was built. You are welcome to bring your own wine to accompany dinner. If you prefer to eat out, try the Foresters Arms, just a two-minute walk away. There are eight classic gardens in South Somerset. Wells and Glastonbury are within easy touring distance, as is the Dorset Coast. *Directions:* From Yeovil, take the A30 (Crewkerne road) for 2 miles to the Yeovil Court Hotel. Turn immediately left at the signpost for East Coker, North Coker, and Hardington. Pass the Foresters Arms, and Holywell House is the next driveway on the right.

HOLYWELL HOUSE
Owners: Jackie & Ronald Somerville
Holywell
East Coker
Yeovil
Somerset BA22 9NQ, England
Tel: (01935) 862612 Fax: (01935) 863035
3 rooms, 2 en suite
From £25 per person
Closed Christmas & New Year
Children welcome

Anthony's forbears have farmed hereabouts for over 300 years and he continues in the family tradition. When Alison and Anthony married they knocked two small cottages into one and added on to the rear to form a spacious home with gardens terracing down to fields and the most spectacular view across the sky-wide fens to Ely Cathedral, a building so large that it dwarfs the little market town that surrounds it. This captivating vista is enjoyed by the very spacious guest bedrooms which occupy wings at either end of the house. At night the cathedral is floodlit and presents a spectacular sight. The bedrooms are light and fresh, with white walls, flowered drapes, pretty bedspreads, and immaculate en-suite bathrooms. Breakfast is the only meal served round the lovely old table in the beamed dining room and guests often dine at The Anchor in Sutton Gault or The Fire Engine House in Ely which serves traditional Fenland food such as smoked eel and pheasant. Cambridge, whose university complex spans over 700 years of history, is a big draw for visitors who stroll through its college courtyards, explore its ancient alleys, and punt or row under the willow trees that line the River Cam. Among Ely's narrow streets are the house where Cromwell lived, Goldsmith's tower and museum, and the enormous cathedral built in 1083. *Directions:* Take the A10 from Cambridge to Ely, approximately 14 miles, turn right at the roundabout onto the A142 towards Newmarket, and Stuntney is on your right. Lower Road is opposite the church.

FORGE COTTAGE
Owners: Alison & Anthony Morbey
Lower Road
Stuntney, Ely
Cambridgeshire CB7 5TN, England
Tel: (01353) 663275 Fax: (01353) 662260
2 en-suite rooms
From £25 per person
Closed Christmas
Children over 10

Julie Graham provides a sincere and relaxed welcome to Ettington Manor and is happy to show guests around her home which has greatly evolved since its original portion was built as a religious establishment in 1276. The drawing room has the comfiest of feather sofas drawn up around an enormous log-burning fireplace. In the adjacent dining room Julie serves dinner by prior arrangement at 7:30 pm, or a pre-theater supper at 6 pm. Three bedrooms are attractively furnished with new pine furniture and each has a modern, en-suite shower room. The fourth is particularly dramatic, with a four-poster bed sitting center stage beneath a high-beamed ceiling and a snug window seat curving round a stone-mullioned window. Ettington Manor is just 5 miles from Stratford-upon-Avon and 10 miles from Warwick Castle. Ragley Hall, Kenilworth, the Cotswolds, and an abundance of National Trust properties are nearby. *Directions:* Ettington is on the A422 Banbury to Stratford-upon-Avon road. At the center of the village turn south into Rogers Lane and Ettington Manor is the first driveway on your right.

ETTINGTON MANOR
Owner: Julie Graham
Ettington
Stratford-upon-Avon
Warwickshire CV37 7SX, England
Tel & fax: (01789) 740216
4 en-suite rooms
From £30 per person
Open March to November
Credit cards: MC, VS
Children over 12
No-smoking house
Wolsey Lodge

Places to Stay

Over 500 years ago this tiny cottage in this quiet Cotswold village was home to the parish priest and today is a welcoming bed and breakfast. The front door opens into the large guest sitting room where a lovely Welsh dresser holds an array of unusual green-and-white china and the breakfast room whose massive inglenook fireplace is decorated with country knickknacks. An old lamp hangs over a large round table where guests gather for breakfast which consists of their choice of traditional bacon and eggs or smoked haddock and kippers. The free-range eggs come from the farm next door and honey from Jan's bees. The three guest bedrooms found at the top of the narrow stairs have lots of simple country charm and each has its own bathroom. A double room has old pine furniture while the large twin has roses peeking in at the window and a view across the fields. Above the stable a one-bedroom self-contained flat is available for bed and breakfast or self catering. Husband David, a banker mason, has carved new stone-mullioned windows for the cottage. Exploring the Cotswolds with their rolling hills and pretty villages is most enjoyable, but guests also love shopping for clothes and antiques, and visiting gardens such as those at Kiftsgate and Hidcote. *Directions:* Take the Cotswold villages of Chipping Norton, Stow-on-the-Wold, and Moreton in Marsh as a triangle on the map and the small village of Evenlode is at the center of the triangle. Twostones is next to the church.

TWOSTONES
Owners: Jan & David Wright
Evenlode
Moreton in Marsh
Gloucestershire GL56 0NY, England
Tel: (01608) 651104
3 rooms, 2 en suite
From £20 per person
Open all year
Children over 10

Hyde Farm House was once the principal farm on the Frampton estate. When the estate was sold Frampton Manor was transported stone by stone to America and the farmhouse fell upon sad times, being rescued by John and Jan who took five years to restore it to the glorious home you see today. The minimum of regimentation is the order of the day, so guests can dine at the time of their choosing and while John cooks, Jan (he hails from Norway) looks after guests, seating them either at the long table in the dining room or in the conservatory overlooking the garden. Guests are encouraged to bring their own wine. Strains of classical music accompany dinner and coffee in the most inviting of drawing rooms. Staffordshire flatback figures (Napoleon, Dick Whittington, and Queen Victoria amongst them) line the staircase which leads to the delightful bedrooms. Chatsworth is a particularly elegant room with its draped bed and large bathroom. This rural corner of Dorset is Thomas Hardy country, set between Maiden Newton (Chalk Newton) and Frampton (Scrimpton) and just 7 miles from the sea at Abbotsbury. It is an easy drive to over 20 gardens and 15 National Trust properties. Bring your rod and enjoy Hyde Farm House's private fishing. *Directions:* Take the A37 from Dorchester towards Yeovil for 5 miles and turn left on the A356 (Crewkerne road) into Frampton. Pass the church on your right, the village hall your left, and Hyde Farm House is on your left after 500 yards.

HYDE FARM HOUSE
Owners: John Saunders & Jan Faye-Schjoll
Dorchester Road
Frampton
nr Dorchester
Dorset DT2 9NG, England
Tel: (01300) 320272
3 en-suite rooms
From £25 per person
Open all year
Children over 12

When Mary and Tony Dakin bought The Old Parsonage at an auction, it was in a sad state of disrepair and they have put a great deal of work into making it the lovely home you see today. In the days when clerics were men of substance, there were six servants for the house and garden, but now its just Mary, Tony, their two young sons, and the tractor-mower. In the morning, Tony cooks breakfast while Mary assists guests. Typical of grand Georgian houses, the rooms are tall and spacious and the Dakins have furnished them in a most delightful manner. Two of the bedrooms have double-bedded four-posters while the third is a spacious twin-bedded room. One of the four-poster rooms has a shower room while the other two rooms have bathrooms with large tubs. Tony is a keen gardener and the sunny conservatory is always full of plants. He is also passionate about photography and has framed photos of longtime village residents lining the hallway and historic Frant pictures in the dining room. Frant is a most attractive village set round a green, with two pubs and a restaurant, Bassetts, where guests usually go for dinner. Information folders in the bedrooms give details on the 15 houses, castles, and gardens to visit in the area. London is a 40-minute train ride from Frant station. *Directions:* From Tunbridge Wells, take the A267 south for 2½ miles to Frant. Turn left at the 30 mph Frant sign, and The Old Parsonage is on your left, just before the church.

THE OLD PARSONAGE
Owners: Mary & Tony Dakin
Church Lane
Frant, Tunbridge Wells
Kent TN3 9DX, England
Tel & fax: (01892) 750773
3 en-suite rooms
From £28 per person
Open all year
Credit cards: MC, VS
Children welcome

The soothing sound of water splashing down the mill race is the only sound that breaks the countryside peace and quiet when you stay at Maplehurst Mill, the site of a mill since 1309. Heather feels that eating here is an integral part of the stay and guests dine by candlelight in the ancient miller's house with its beams and inglenook fireplace. Bottomend, a ground-floor bedroom, sits directly above the mill race and its windows open onto the moss-covered millwheel. Topend, at the top of the mill, has a beamed bathroom and the four-poster room which overlooks the meadows has its bed strategically placed on the sloping floor. The room across the garden in the stables lacks the warm country character of those in the mill. A heated swimming pool overlooks the fields. Idencroft Herb Gardens are just round the corner and Brattle Farm, an old-fashioned working farm, is an excellent choice for those who have visited all Kent's castles, gardens, and stately homes. *Directions:* From the M20 take the A229 Hastings exit and follow Hastings signs through Maidstone for 12 miles to Staplehurst. At the end of the village turn left into the Frittenden road. After 1¼ miles, opposite a white house, turn right into a narrow lane. At the end turn right and the mill is at the foot of the incline.

MAPLEHURST MILL
Owners: Heather & Kenneth Parker
Mill Lane
Frittenden
Kent TN17 2DT, England
Tel & fax: (01580) 852203
5 en-suite rooms
From £28 per person
Open all year
Credit cards: MC, VS
Children over 12
No-smoking house
Wolsey Lodge

Goldhill Mill (mentioned in the Domesday Book of 1086) was a working mill for over 800 years. The mill wheel still turns behind a glass partition in the kitchen where Shirley chats to guests as she cooks them breakfast. After breakfast, feed your toast to the swans who reside on the millpond. The Coles have compiled a list of recommended restaurants and pubs for dinner, including comments and prices. Two of Shirley's great-great-grandfather's paintings of Egypt hang in the comfortable guests' sitting room—he was the artist on Carter's 1922 expedition which discovered Tutankhamen's tomb. Unlike so many expedition members, he did not succumb to the "curse" and lived into old age—part of which was spent in this house. The bedrooms are very luxurious. Pink has a romantic pastel decor and luxurious bathroom with Jacuzzi tub; Millpool overlooks the millpool and is all lilacs and roses on the wallpaper, drapes, and bedspread; The Four-Poster room overlooks acres of garden towards the tennis court. Across the courtyard are two deluxe self-catering cottages which sleep four to six people. Kent abounds in castles, and stately homes. *Directions:* From Tonbridge, take the A26 towards Maidstone for 2 miles. Turn right down Three Elm Lane, and after 1¼ miles left into the mill's driveway.

GOLDHILL MILL
Owners: Shirley & Vernon Cole
Golden Green
Tonbridge
Kent TN11 0BA, England
Tel: (01732) 851626 Fax: (01732) 851881
3 en-suite rooms
From £35 per person
Closed mid-July to September & New Year
Credit cards: MC, VS
Children over 16
No-smoking house

Set in acres of lovely gardens which include a grass tennis court and heated swimming pool, Ennys is an idyllic, 17th-century manor house set deep in Cornish countryside, 3 miles from St. Michael's Mount. Polished flagstones line the hallway leading to the garden where on fine summer evenings guests gather at 7 o'clock for a chat over sherry before going in to dinner at four little tables set around the fireplace. On cool evenings, drinks are served in the cheery sitting room. Upstairs are three lovely bedrooms, two of them delectable four-posters. Families are welcome in the suites which occupy an adjacent barn—bedrooms here are also delightfully appointed, though without the bric-a-brac that children find so hazardous. St. Michael's Mount is a "must do," as is spending an evening at the open-air Minack theater in Porthcurno. A delightful day trip involves an hour's countryside walk (or a short drive) to the railway station where you take a train to St. Ives to visit the Tate Gallery which displays the work of 20th-century St. Ives artists. *Directions:* From Exeter, take the A30 to Crowlas village which is 4 miles before Penzance. Turn towards Helston, at the roundabout, and at the next roundabout turn left at the signpost for Relubbus. Go through Goldsithney to St. Hilary, and when the Ennys Farm's signpost is on the right, turn left and follow the lane for a mile to the farm.

ENNYS FARM
Owners: Susan & John White
St. Hilary, Goldsithney
Penzance
Cornwall TR20 9BZ, England
Tel: (01736) 740262
5 en-suite rooms
From £20 per person
Closed Christmas
Children welcome in family suites

Sitting beside the village green at the heart of this quiet, unspoilt Cotswold village, The Lamb is a picture-perfect hostelry. Locals gather in the evening in the quaint bar where pride of place is given to a picture gallery of guide dogs for the blind who have been sponsored by patrons' donations. Decked out in pine, the restaurant with its soft-pink decor is most attractive. The menu is à la carte with such dishes as beef Wellington and grilled lamb cutlets with onion sauce. Simpler fare is served in the bar and adjacent buttery. Up the narrow, winding staircase and down twisting, narrow corridors are an array of cottage-style bedrooms, all furnished differently (suitable only for the nimble of foot). Two have intricately carved four-poster beds made by Richard. Thick stone walls with deeply set windows, low ceilings, quaint doors, and beams all add to the old-world feel. The two rooms in the converted stable are not as attractive. Outside is a landscaped garden—the perfect place to enjoy a glass of real ale on a warm summer evening. Most people come here to tour the picturesque Cotswold villages, explore gardens such as Hidcote, and visit Stratford-upon-Avon and Oxford. *Directions:* From the A429 turn into Bourton-on-the-Water, carry on along this road (not into the village), and take the first turn right to Great Rissington.

THE LAMB INN
Owners: Kate & Richard Cleverly
Great Rissington
Bourton-on-the-Water
Gloucestershire GL54 2LD, England
Tel: (01451) 820388 Fax: (01451) 820724
12 en-suite rooms
From £22 per person
Closed Christmas
Credit cards: all major
Children welcome

Church House, a spacious Georgian home, has a sweep of driveway circling to the front door beneath massive copper beeches. To the rear are lawns, sheep pasture, and a helicopter landing pad for those who care to arrive by air. Guests have a high-ceilinged comfortable yellow drawing room where Anna displays her collection of paintings by West-Country artist Reg Gammon. Anna is happy with advance notice to prepare dinner. Guests eat together round the long polished table and you are welcome to bring your own wines. A graceful wooden staircase spirals its way up to the top floor and the homey guestrooms. The largest bedroom has its private bathroom across the hall while the other three rooms have their facilities in the room, artfully concealed behind tall wooden screens. Ask for the one with the view from the loo of Grittleton rooftops. On the landing is an information table showing all the things to do and see in the area, though guests are welcome to spend their days relaxing around the heated swimming pool. Grittleton is well placed to visit Bath, Bristol, Malmesbury, Tetbury, and the picture-perfect village of Castle Combe. Every May the Badminton horse trials are held nearby. *Directions:* Exit the M4 at junction 17, taking the A429 towards Cirencester, and almost immediately (at the crossroads) turn left for the 3½-mile drive to Grittleton. Church House is beside the church.

CHURCH HOUSE
Owners: Anna & Michael Moore
Grittleton
Chippenham
Wiltshire SN14 6AP, England
Tel & fax: (01249) 782562
4 rooms, 3 en suite
From £27.75 per person
Open all year
Children over 12

Surrounded by a sky-wide landscape of fields, this converted 19th-century oast offers spacious accommodation within a half hour's drive of Kent's most celebrated tourist attractions. The lower half of the roundels, where the hops were roasted, has been converted into a spacious sitting room, but, more often than not, guests gather in the open-plan kitchen that was formerly a barn. If you would like to eat in, Ann discusses the menu at length and precedes the four-course meal with drinks in the sitting room. Two bedrooms (a twin and a double) occupy the upper reaches of the roundels and share a well-equipped bathroom. The third bedroom is very large and has its bathroom en suite. Sasha, the friendly golden retriever, is a great favorite with guests. Ann gives her guests lists of places to visit and a map of pubs and restaurants in the area to assist them in making sightseeing and dining decisions. Nearby places of interest include Chartwell (Churchill's home), 13th-century Hever Castle, the onetime home of the Boleyn family, and Penshurst Place, a 14th-century manor house. *Directions:* From Tonbridge, take the A26 towards Maidstone. After the village of Hadlow, pass Leavers Manor Hotel on the right and turn right into Stanford Lane. Leavers Oast is the third driveway on your right.

LEAVERS OAST
Owners: Ann & Denis Turner
Stanford Lane
Hadlow
Kent TN11 0JN, England
Tel & fax: (01732) 850924
3 rooms, 1 en suite
From £25 per person
Closed Christmas & New Year
Children over 12
No-smoking house

There are many good reasons to visit Leicestershire and this exceptional home at the edge of a peaceful village with many picturesque thatched cottages is one of them. Here old furniture is gleamingly polished, the windows sparkle, and everything is in apple-pie order. The evening sun streams into the drawing room where books on stately homes and castles invite browsing. Breakfast is served in a small dining room with a long trestle table. If there are several people for dinner, Raili (who grew up in Finland) sets the elegant table in the large dining room and serves a variety of meals using organic vegetables from her garden. The principal bedroom has en-suite facilities, while the other guestrooms share a large family bathroom. Bedrooms have televisions and someone is always on hand to make a pot of tea. A three-day Christmas program gives guests the opportunity to experience a quiet, traditional English country Christmas—visits to the hunt and the midnight carol service are highlights. Nearby are a great many stately homes (Burghley House and Rockingham Castle, for instance), lots of antique shops, the vast expanse of Rutland Water, cathedrals at Ely and Peterborough, historic towns (Stamford and Uppingham), and ancient villages. *Directions:* From Uppingham take the A47 and turn left at East Norton for Hallaton. Drive through the village and The Old Rectory is next to the church.

THE OLD RECTORY
Owners: Raili & Tom Fraser
Hallaton
Market Harborough
Leicestershire LE16 8TY, England
Tel: (01858) 555350
3 rooms, 1 en suite
From £26 per person
Open all year
Children over 7
Wolsey Lodge

Sandbarn Farm was originally part of the Lucy family's estate at nearby Charlecote. During the 1980s this 16th-century farmhouse was extensively modernized and now it is home to Helen and Paul Waterworth who offer guests a quiet countryside retreat just ten minutes' drive from Stratford-upon-Avon. Guests have a snug television lounge and eat breakfast together round the dining-room table. A pub in the village serves meals, but Helen is also happy to suggest restaurants in Stratford. Under the eaves, two large bedrooms can either be twin-bedded or have their beds zipped together as king-sized, and each has a spacious bathroom and additional single bedroom (no reduction for children). A third bedroom has its private bathroom across the hallway. The Lucy family have resided across the fields at Charlcote Park since 1204 in a gracious home which was modernized during the 19th century. You can tour the Victorian kitchens and grand rooms and enjoy beautiful walks through vast acres of parkland. While Stratford-upon-Avon is a must to visit, also remember to wander into Warwick, with its mixture of Georgian and old timber houses and magnificent castle. *Directions:* Exit the M40 at junction 15, and take the A46, Stratford road. At the next roundabout, fork left on the A439 signposted Stratford Town Centre. Turn left at a small crossroads (with a large Mercedes showroom) to Hampton Lucy, and Sandbarn Farm is on the right after 1½ miles.

SANDBARN FARM
Owners: Helen & Paul Waterworth
Hampton Lucy
Warwickshire CV35 8AU, England
Tel: (01789) 842280
3 en-suite rooms
From £25 per person
Closed Christmas
Children over 5

Surrounded by lush green fields, Greenlooms Cottage offers a quiet countryside location just 5 miles from the heart of medieval Chester. The cottage was the hedger-and-ditcher's cottage on the Duke of Westminster's Eaton estate. Hezekiah, the last incumbent, lived here for many years with his sister Miriam who raised pigs and geese. Now Greenlooms is home to Deborah and Peter Newman who have sympathetically extended and modernized the cottage, while keeping all its lovely old features such as the low beamed ceilings and the pump in the garden. Step through the front door into the old-fashioned pine country kitchen where Deborah serves breakfast. Through the snug television room you come to the cottagey little bedrooms. For dinner, Deborah usually suggests the Grosvenor Arms in Aldford or dining in the atmospheric bar at nearby Willington Hall. Rather than looking for parking in the center of Chester, drive to the Park and Ride from where a shuttle bus transports you into town (runs every ten minutes till 6 pm). Conwy Castle and Bodnant Gardens in Wales are a very popular day trip. *Directions:* From Chester take the A41 (Whitchurch road) south for 2 miles, and turn left at Whitehouse Antiques (before the Black Dog pub). Follow the road through the village for 1½ miles, turn right into Martins Lane, and Greenlooms Cottage is on your right, after less than a mile.

GREENLOOMS COTTAGE
Owners: Deborah & Peter Newman
Hargrave
Chester
Cheshire CH3 7RY, England
Tel: (01829) 781475
2 en-suite rooms
From £17.50 per person
Open all year
Children welcome

Christine and David Cooper have lovingly and with great imagination converted this mill, barn, and mill house (mentioned in the Domesday Book of 1086) into a secluded hideaway set amid woodland, water, and pasture. In the mill the Dutch-door entrance leads into a sitting room with two round grinding stones on the floor and antique pulleys and gears above. From here separate steep, narrow staircases lead up to two very tiny bedrooms (small suitcases only). Although little, each bedroom is bright and cheery with sun streaming in from the overhead skylight. The bathrooms are reached by very steep, ladder-like steps down from the bedrooms (definitely not a place to stay for the infirm). The adjacent old wooden barn is all beams and coziness. Downstairs there are a sitting room and small bedroom and up the narrow stairs low doors lead to two additional small bedrooms. The romantic four-poster room's bed is made partially from the timbers of a haywagon. In the double bedroom you have to bend almost double to duck beneath a beam to enter the bathroom. Breakfast is served in the Coopers' mill house. A light supper tray can be ordered. *Directions:* Take the A264 from Tunbridge Wells, then go 1 mile south on the B2026 towards Hartfield. Turn left just past Perryhill Nurseries on the farm track and keep right at the Y.

BOLEBROKE MILL
Owners: Christine & David Cooper
Edenbridge Road
Hartfield
Sussex TN7 4JP, England
Tel: (01892) 770425
5 en-suite rooms
From £26.50 per person
Credit cards: all major
Open March to November
Children over 7
No-smoking house

It was love at first sight when I came upon Carr Head Farm sitting high above Hathersage village with steep crags and windswept heather moors as a backdrop. The garden presents a large flagstone patio, a profusion of flowers nestled in little niches in the terraces leading down to a sweeping lawn, and the most spectacular view across this beautiful Derbyshire valley. The beauty of Mary Bailey's gardens is matched by the loveliness of her home where everything has been done with caring and impeccable taste. The beamed dining room is furnished in period style with groupings of tables and chairs where guests gather for breakfast, the only meal served. The adjacent drawing room is very elegant in blues and creams, a bowl of sweets sitting on the coffee table next to a stack of interesting books. The two lovely bedrooms have en-suite facilities. The four-poster room offers beautiful views of the valley. The Peak District with its picturesque villages, stone-walled fields, and dramatic dales is on your doorstep, as are Haddon Hall and Chatsworth House. *Directions:* Exit the M1 at junction 29 towards Baslow where you take the A623 to the B6001, through Grindleford to Hathersage. At the junction with the main road, turn right up the village, left into School Lane, and first left. Just before the church (Little John of Robin Hood fame has his grave in the churchyard) turn right up Church Bank to the farm.

CARR HEAD FARM
Owners: Mary & Michael Bailey
Church Bank
Hathersage
Sheffield S30 1BR, England
Tel & fax: (01433) 650383
2 en-suite rooms
From £22 per person
Closed Christmas
Children over 12

Sheltered in a gentle fold of the hills beneath the spectacular crags of Haytor Rocks, Haytor Vale is a quiet village containing little cottages and The Rock Inn. With its wooden beams and huge open fireplace, the inn has a cozy, traditional ambiance. Bedrooms are named after horses that have won the Grand National: Lovely has an old oak four-poster bed and a dark beamed ceiling, Master Robert and Freebooter are rooms with sloping ceilings and large private bathrooms. A relatively small supplement is charged for these deluxe rooms, and it is well worth paying. All the bedrooms have television (including a movie channel), tea and coffee, telephone, and a mini-bar. The food here is delightful: bar meals range from traditional roasts to curries (the desserts are especially tempting), while the candlelit restaurant serves a set-price dinner with a wide variety of choices for each course. From the giant rocky outcrop of neighboring Haytor Rocks you can see the vast extent of Dartmoor National Park, the Teign estuary, and the rolling hills of southern Devon. The nearby quarry supplied the stone used for building London Bridge, which now resides in America. *Directions:* Take the M5 from Exeter which joins the A38, Plymouth road, then the A382 to Bovey Tracey. At the first roundabout turn left and follow the road up to Haytor and cross a cattle grid onto the moor. After passing an old gas station, turn left into Haytor Vale.

THE ROCK INN
Owner: Christopher Graves
Haytor Vale
Newton Abbot
Devon TQ13 9XP, England
Tel: (01364) 661305 Fax: (01364) 661242
10 rooms, 8 en suite
From £35.50 per person
Open all year
Credit cards: all major
Children welcome

Jane Harman is an enthusiastic gardener and loves to host fellow enthusiasts who come to tour the many lovely gardens in Kent. Guests have their own entry which leads to a charmingly furnished, low-beamed sitting room with walls lined with interesting books and a brick floor topped by a pretty rug. In the adjacent dining room gleaming copper and brass accent the huge inglenook fireplace. Guests dine together round the polished table by the soft glow of candlelight. Upstairs, creaking, crooked floors lead to the bedrooms and I particularly admired the spacious Blue Room. The Middle Room's bathroom is next door to it, but plans are afoot to break through the walls, so it may be en suite by the time you visit. Downstairs, a spacious twin room can accommodate guests who have difficulty walking. Jane has compiled a folder on the many places of interest to visit (you'll need to stay a month if you plan on visiting them all). Another folder covers the plethora of gardens, amongst the more famous of which are Sissinghurst, Doddington, Mount Ephraim, Pashley Manor, Goodnestone, and Great Dixter. Guests often make day trips to London. *Directions:* Exit the M20 at junction 8 towards Leeds Castle. Go through Leeds village to the A274, turn left and continue through Sutton Valence and 1 mile beyond Headcorn to the crossroads. Turn right signposted Waterman Quarter and Vine Farm is on the left after ¾ mile.

VINE FARM
Owners: Jane & Tim Harman
Headcorn
Kent TN27 9JJ, England
Tel: (01622) 890203 Fax: (01622) 891819
3 en-suite rooms
From £19.50 per person
Open all year
Credit cards: all major
Children over 10
No-smoking house

Cobblestones border the main street of Helperby, a village where the number of shops (four) just outnumbers the pubs. Fronting onto the narrow lane that leads to the church, Brafferton Hall was built in the 1740s as the dower house to the much grander Helperby Hall which lies at the opposite end of the village. Now it is home to Sue and John White who find that their home's spacious, well-proportioned rooms are perfect for entertaining guests country-house style. Sue and John have an easy, friendly manner, so it a pleasure to join them in the garden for pre-dinner drinks, dine with them, and chat afterwards over coffee and chocolates in the drawing room. (Sue thoughtfully feeds children an early supper so that they can be tucked up in bed by dinner time.) Upstairs, the pine room is named after its furniture and has its own private bathroom. A large double room overlooks the garden and another has views across to the village schoolhouse—both have en-suite bathrooms. Down the hall, a snug single with en-suite shower room is perfect for a child. Brafferton Hall is perfectly located for exploring not only the Yorkshire dales and moors, but also Rievaulx and Fountains abbeys, Castle Howard, Shandy Hall, Whitby and the coast, Harrogate, and York. *Directions:* Leave the A1 at Boroughbridge and follow the Easingwold road to Helperby. Take the first turning on the right after the 30 mph sign and Brafferton Hall is on your left after 100 yards.

BRAFFERTON HALL
Owners: Sue & John White
Helperby, York
Yorkshire Y06 2NZ, England
Tel & fax: (01423) 360352
4 rooms, 3 en suite
From £30 per person
Open all year
Credit cards: all major
Children welcome
Wolsey Lodge

East Peterel Field Farm offers spectacular views of rolling countryside with hardly another building in sight, yet you are just over a mile from the delightful market town of Hexham, and 2 miles from Hadrian's Wall, the bleak, northernmost outpost of the Roman Empire. The glory of East Peterel Field Farm is its vast country kitchen where guests enjoy breakfast at the long trestle table in front of tall windows which frame the idyllic countryside views. Susan loves to cook, so specials such as salmon cakes and kedgeree are often served at breakfast time (she often gives cookery demonstrations or invites guest chefs to demonstrate their arts). Guests dine together round the dining-room table and are encouraged to bring their own wine to accompany their meal. If she has a large dinner party, Susan serves coffee in the lovely drawing room, but for smaller parties she utilizes the snug, a most attractive room full of comfortable chairs where a log fire bids a cheery welcome. The master bedroom is vast, the twin room lovely, and the small double has its bathroom just next door. David runs a small stud farm where he breeds and raises thoroughbreds—his dream is to breed a Derby winner. Hadrian's Wall is a great attraction hereabouts. The beautiful Northumbrian coast with all its castles is about a 40-mile drive away. *Directions:* From Hexham, turn into Blanchland Road, at the Tap and Spile pub, bear right at the Y for 1 mile, and take the first farm track to your right after the Black House restaurant.

EAST PETEREL FIELD FARM
Owners: Susan & David Carr
Hexham
Northumberland NE46 2JT, England
Tel: (01434) 607209 Fax: (01434) 601753
3 rooms, 2 en suite
From £23 per person
Open all year
Children welcome

This timbered pink house and its black-painted wooden barn hug a quiet country road on the edge of the peaceful Suffolk village of Higham. Meg Parker, with her gentle dalmatian Percy at her heels, offers a warm smile and a sincere welcome to her home, quickly putting visitors at ease. Meg leads her guests to the lovely drawing room and then escorts them up the broad staircase to their rooms. Breakfast is enjoyed around the large dining-room table, and, since it is the only meal served, she is happy to offer advice on where to dine, often suggesting The Angel at Stoke by Nayland. Bedrooms vary in size from large twin-bedded rooms to a cozy double room, in the oldest part of the house, with an en-suite bathroom. Outside, Meg's large garden is carefully tended and stretches towards the River Brett where a punt and a canoe are available for guests' use. The narrow Brett soon becomes the broader Stour and you can punt/paddle upstream for a picnic and idly drift home or go downstream to Stratford St. Mary and work off a lunch at The Swan by making your way back upstream. An unheated swimming pool is tucked into one sheltered corner of the garden and a well kept tennis court occupies another. A highlight of a stay here is to visit Flatford, immortalized in the paintings of John Constable. *Directions:* Leave the A12 between Colchester and Ipswich at Stratford St. Mary. The Old Vicarage is 1 mile to the west next to the church.

THE OLD VICARAGE
Owners: Meg & John Parker
Higham
Colchester
Suffolk CO7 6JY, England
Tel: (0120) 6337248
3 rooms, 1 en suite
From £24 per person
Open all year
Children welcome
Wolsey Lodge

Pam and Roger Laidler offer a hospitable welcome to their 350-year-old picture-book thatched cottage, Quantock House, nestled in Holford village beneath the Quantock Hills. Breakfast and a good-value-for-money dinner are served in the large beamed sitting/dining room, warmed by a wood-burning stove set in the large inglenook fireplace. Bedrooms are small and cottagey with either a snug, en-suite shower room or a bathroom next to bedroom. I particularly enjoyed the downstairs bedroom with its little window seat, small shower room, and pine bed topped by a handmade quilt. While everything is quaint and pretty, I found the upstairs bathroom dated in style. Pam loves needlework and there are framed pictures of her and her grandmother's handiwork throughout the house. Coleridge lived in the adjacent village of Nether Stowey when he wrote *The Ancient Mariner*, and guests often tour his cottage. Wordsworth also lived nearby at Alfoxton House which is now a hotel. Nearby Kilve Beach is famous for its fossilized ammonites and the Laidlers have a particularly large one on the back terrace. This is an exceptional walking area and Pam and Roger can suggest pretty walks that last between an hour and a day. *Directions:* From Bridgwater take the A39 (Minehead road) for 12 miles to Holford, where you turn left between the Texaco station and the Plough Inn—Quantock House is on your right.

QUANTOCK HOUSE
Owners: Pam & Roger Laidler
Holford
Bridgwater
Somerset TA5 1RY, England
Tel: (01278) 741439
3 en-suite rooms
From £19 per person
Open all year
Children welcome
No-smoking house

Horsleygate Hall nestles in the sheltered Cordwell valley at the edge of the Peak District National Park. The hall was built in 1783 as a farmhouse and later extended in 1836 and Margaret and Robert have been careful to preserve all its old features such as the old farmhouse kitchen with its blackened Yorkshire range, flagstone floors, and the old pine woodwork and doors. Guests have a comfortable, homey sitting room and enjoy breakfast in the old schoolroom next door. Visitors often go to the Royal Oak in Millthorpe or the Robin Hood in Holmesfield for dinner. The attractive, spacious bedrooms enjoy views of the magnificent garden and superb Peak District scenery. The lovely garden contains many enchanting treasures: terraces, flower-filled borders, rock gardens, pools, and woodland paths. A grand garden on an infinitely larger scale surrounds Chatsworth House, the enormous home of the Duke and Duchess of Devonshire, which is full of opulent rooms and priceless paintings and furniture. Haddon Hall, a romantic, 14th-century manor house, has a fragrant rose garden. Bakewell, Ilam, Edensor, Hartington, Ashford-in-the-Water, and Eyam are particularly attractive villages in this area. *Directions:* Leave the M1 motorway at junction 29 into Chesterfield where you take the B6051 (Hathersage) through Barlow and Millthorpe, then take the first turn right (Horsleygate Lane) and immediately left into Horsleygate Hall's driveway.

HORSLEYGATE HALL
Owners: Margaret & Robert Ford
Horsleygate Lane
Holmesfield, near Chesterfield
Derbyshire S18 5WD, England
Tel: (01142) 890333
3 rooms, 1 en suite
From £17 per person
Open all year
Children over 5

The first thing you notice when you come through Woodhayes' front door is the portraits, huge paintings that sometimes stretch from floor to ceiling. Once you have made yourself at home in this friendly house you may be inclined, as I was, to do a "who's who" of Noel's forbears, ascertaining how the congenial pictures in your room are related to all the others. Guests dine by candlelight round the polished dining-room table in what was at one time the home's kitchen—hence the flagstone floors and huge inglenook fireplace which now contains a wood-burning stove. The twin-bedded room at the front of the house has commanding views across the valley while the four-poster room overlooks the rose garden at the side of the house, and both have en-suite bathrooms. A single bedroom has its private bathroom down the hall. Dumpdon Celtic hill fort rises behind the house and beyond lies the rolling green of the Blackdown hills, a wonderful place for walking. Nearby Honiton is the historic center for lace making and a small museum chronicles the industry's history and development. A 20-minute drive brings you to the Victorian resort of Sidmouth and Beer, a fishing village in a little bay. *Directions:* Woodhayes is prominently visible on high ground 1½ miles northeast of Honiton. Take the Dunkeswell road, cross the River Otter, and take the first turn right. Woodhayes is the first drive on the left.

WOODHAYES
Owners: Christy & Noel Page Turner
Honiton
Devon EX14 0TP, England
Tel: (01404) 42011
3 rooms, 2 en suite
From £31 per person
Open March to mid-December
Children over 15
Wolsey Lodge

Sitting at the heart of the peaceful village of Hornton, the 17th-century Manor House is the exquisite home of Vicki and Malcolm Patrick and their three children. The elegant drawing room is set aside for guests' use and meals are taken in the beautifully appointed beamed dining room. Winter, decked out in soft tones of peach, is a delightful bedroom. Sweet peas decorate the bedlinen in the Crow's Nest, an aptly named, snug attic room with exposed stone walls and a huge beam running across its floor. Across the courtyard, part of the stables has been converted into an adorable, two-bedroom, one-bath cottage which can be rented as self-catering or on a bed-and-breakfast basis. Vicki is happy to prepare dinner or directs guests to one of the numerous village pubs that serves excellent food. Guests are welcome to swim in the swimming pool. The Manor House is ideally situated for visiting Stratford-upon-Avon, Warwick Castle, and the Cotswold villages. Upton House, with its amazing collections of old masters paintings, Brussels tapestries, porcelain figures, and 18th-century furniture, is popular, as is the glorious Elizabethan home Charlcote and its surrounding park. *Directions:* From Banbury take the B4100 signposted Gaydon for ½ mile, then turn left for Horley and Hornton. In Horley turn right to Hornton and in 2 miles turn left for Hornton. Drive down the hill and The Manor House is on the left, opposite the village school.

THE MANOR HOUSE
Owners: Vicki & Malcolm Patrick
The Green
Hornton, Banbury
Oxon OX15 6BZ, England
Tel: (01295) 670386
4 rooms, 2 en suite
From £27.50 per person
Open all year
Children welcome

Behind the tile-hung façade of Rixons lies a home that dates back to Tudor times, full of beams and low ceilings, with an inglenook fireplace and a snug, paneled study. Jean and Geoffrey dine with their visitors at the long refectory table, joining them afterwards for coffee and conversation round the fire. The galleried guestroom is open to the rafters with its bedroom downstairs and a sitting room and the bathroom on the balcony above. Honey-colored beams, country-pine furniture, and sprigged bedcovers make the twin-bedded room, tucked under the eaves, a delight. Horsted Keynes has a lovely old church built as a replica of one in Cahagnes, France by a Norman nobleman after the Battle of Hastings. By appointment you can visit The Forge, an adjacent museum containing artifacts of North American Plains Indians. On weekends and in the summer vintage steam trains run between Horsted Keynes and Sheffield Park which is especially beautiful in spring when the rhododendrons and azaleas are in bloom. *Directions:* From East Grinstead (adjacent to Gatwick) take the A22 south through Forest Row and beyond for 2 miles to the Roebuck Hotel where you turn right for Danehill. At Danehill turn right and follow signs for Horsted Keynes. Rixons is opposite the post office.

RIXONS
Owners: Jean & Geoffrey Pink
Lewes Road
Horsted Keynes
West Sussex RH17 7DP, England
Tel: (01825) 790453 Fax: (01825) 740144
  (attn. Rixons)
2 en-suite rooms
From £27 per person
Closed Christmas & New Year
Children over 12
No-smoking house
Wolsey Lodge

In 1248 John D'Jeu came from France to establish a farm here and over the years the locals corrupted the name to Jews Farm. You enter the house through a decorative, warm-peach hallway which leads into the lofty dining room with its walk-in fireplace, long, polished oak table, sturdy chairs, and small-paned windows overlooking an idyllic green valley. The adjacent drawing room enjoys the same view though the focus of the room is the enormous fireplace where a blazing log fire crackles. Sarah and John are the most welcoming of hosts and if guests do not wish to eat in, they direct them to nearby country pubs and restaurants that they enjoy. Upstairs the bedrooms are decorated to the highest of standards. The Blue Room with its lovely brass-and-iron double bed has an en-suite bathroom, as has the Green Room with its four-poster bed. The remaining twin-bedded room has a private bathroom. This unspoilt region of narrow lanes bordering green fields which contrast with open moorlands, with picture-postcard villages nestling in sheltered valleys, is relatively free of holiday traffic. *Directions:* Leave the M5 at exit 25 (Taunton) and follow signs for Barnstaple (B3227) to Wiveliscombe where you turn right at the traffic lights then right at the White Hart pub signposted Huish Champflower. After 2 miles, at the top of a steep hill, turn right down a narrow lane and Jews Farm House is the second turning on the left.

JEWS FARM HOUSE
Owners: Sarah & John Fox
Huish Champflower
Wiveliscombe, Taunton
Somerset TA4 2HL, England
Tel: (01984) 624218
3 rooms, 2 en suite
From £30 per person
Closed December & January
Children over 10
Wolsey Lodge

Set in a valley carved by a stream rushing down from high, bleak moorlands, Hutton le Hole is a cluster of pale stone houses, a picturesque village in the heart of the spectacular North Yorkshire Moors National Park. The lintel above the Hammer and Hand's doorway declares the date of the house, built as a beer house for the iron workers, as 1784. Now it is home to Ann, a journalist, and John, once a London policeman, and their family who happily welcome guests to their bed and breakfast. John's passion for cricket explains the old cricket prints hanging in the dining room and the bar. Tucked behind the dining room (dinner is available every night) is a minute bar offering just enough room for a drink before dinner. The gentle tick of a huge grandfather clock and the crackle of a blazing log fire welcome you to the sitting room. A steep, narrow staircase leads to three snug bedrooms, each prettily decorated to give a feeling of light and warmth. Ann finds that Cook's Cabin, a pocket-sized attic room with heavy ships' beams supporting the steeply sloping ceiling, is very popular despite the inconvenience of negotiating a narrow, twisting staircase to use its bathroom on the floor below. Hutton le Hole houses the Ryedale Folk Museum which is well worth a visit. York is less than an hour's drive away. *Directions:* Take the A170 from Thirsk towards Pickering. The left-hand turn to Hutton le Hole is signposted just after Kirbymoorside. The Hammer and Hand is at the heart of the village.

HAMMER AND HAND GUEST HOUSE
Owners: Ann, Michael & John Wilkins
Hutton le Hole
York
Yorkshire YO6 6UA, England
Tel: (01751) 417300
3 rooms, 2 en suite
From £20 per person
Closed Christmas
Children welcome

Lavenham with its lovely timbered buildings, ancient guildhall, and spectacular church is the most attractive village in Suffolk. The Great House on the corner of the market square, a 15th-century building with an imposing 18th-century façade, houses a French restaurant-with-rooms run by Martine and Regis Crepy. Dinner is served in the oak-beamed dining room with candlelight and soft music and is particularly good value for money from Monday to Friday when a fixed-price menu is offered. On Saturday you dine from the à-la-carte menu and on Sunday evenings the restaurant is closed. In summer you can dine al fresco in the flower-filled courtyard. There are four large bedrooms, all with a lounge or a sitting area. Architecturally the rooms are divinely old-world, with sloping plank floors, creaking floorboards, little windows, and a plethora of beams. Enjoy them for their size and age, not for their decor which is eclectically homey and not particularly spiffy. The bathrooms are small and somewhat dated. Enjoy the village in the peace and quiet of the evening after the throng of daytime summer visitors has departed. Next door, Little Hall is furnished in turn-of-the-century style and is open as a museum. Farther afield are other historic villages such as Kersey and Long Melford, and Constable's Flatford Mill. *Directions*: Lavenham is on the A1141 between Bury St. Edmunds and Hadleigh.

THE GREAT HOUSE   **NEW**
Owners: Martine & Regis Crepy
Market Place
Lavenham
Suffolk CO10 9QZ, England
Tel: (01787) 247431 Fax: (01787) 248007
4 en-suite rooms
From £34 per person
Closed January
Credit cards: all major
Children welcome

John claims that he would still be wandering the world (something he had done for over three years) if he had not met Hazel who brought him back to live in the Lake District valley where she was raised. Together they have restored a roadside farm, providing guest accommodation in the farmhouse and transforming the barn into a tea room and restaurant. Flagstone floors, beamed ceilings, and old fireplaces are the order of the day in the farm. Hazel prepares a set, four-course dinner, but if you prefer a lighter, less formal meal, walk across to the barn where little tables and chairs are arranged in the old cow stalls, specials are posted on the board, and main courses include quiche, fish, and steak. Upstairs two of the country-cozy bedrooms offer zip-link beds and en-suite bathrooms. A snug double has an en-suite shower room. All have delightful countyside views. New House Farm sits amid the rugged scenery which has made the Lake District such a draw for centuries. Follow the country lane to Crummock Water and Buttermere from where the road winds and twists over the fells to Rosthwaite, Grange, and Keswick. *Directions:* From exit 40 on the M6 take the A66 past Keswick, and turn left onto the B5292 to Lorton. Follow signs for Buttermere and New House Farm is on your left after half a mile.

NEW HOUSE FARM   **NEW**
Owners: Hazel & John Hatch
Lorton near Cockermouth
Cumbria CA13 9UU, England
Tel & fax: (01900) 85404
3 en-suite rooms
From £30 per person
Open all year
Children over 12
No-smoking house

The magnificent scenery of the Lake District, the Yorkshire Dales, and Hadrian's Wall are within easy driving distance of Hipping Hall, so visitors can easily justify a stay of several days in Jocelyn Ruffle and Ian Bryant's comfortable home. Guests help themselves to pre-dinner drinks from the honesty bar in the conservatory which links the main part of the house to the Great Hall where dinner is served. A soaring, beamed ceiling and a broad-oak-plank floor provide an impressive setting for the excellent five-course meal served around one large table where guests are looked after by Ian while Jos creates in the kitchen. Ian selects wine to complement each course. The bedrooms are named after local hills and dales, and all are comfortably and very tastefully furnished, often with lovely old pieces bought at local auctions. Each has its own sparkling new, well equipped bathroom. The 3 acres of garden are a delight and feature a large expanse of lawn set up for croquet and a kitchen garden which provides many of the vegetables enjoyed at dinner. Two suites, named Emily and Charlotte after the Brontë sisters who attended school in Cowan Bridge, occupy a courtyard cottage. They each have a kitchen and living room downstairs, bedroom and bathroom upstairs. *Directions:* Leave the M6 at junction 36 and follow the A65 through Kirkby Lonsdale towards Skipton. Hipping Hall is on the left, 3 miles after Kirkby Lonsdale.

HIPPING HALL
Owners: Jocelyn Ruffle & Ian Bryant
Cowan Bridge
Kirkby Lonsdale
Cumbria LA6 2JJ, England
Tel: (015242) 71187 Fax: (015242) 72452
5 en-suite rooms (& 2 suites)
From £39 per person
Open March to November
Credit cards: MC, VS
Children over 12

As long ago as 1290 Penisale market was held here, but by the 1980s, all that was left of the community of Penisale was the shell of a farm and an ancient barn at the end of a rutted track. A local entrepreneur demolished the barn and incorporated its aged beams and stones into his vision of an Elizabethan farmhouse which he intended to be the center of a leisure complex. The venture went bankrupt and was purchased by Ann and Philip Unitt. They have done the most magnificent job of removing the "Las Vegas" aspects of the conversion and making this one of the premier bed-and-breakfast establishments in South Yorkshire. Splurge and request the Alderman's Suite and you're treated to a queen-sized bed set in an alcove beneath massive beams and a decadent bathroom complete with enormous tub. The three other bedrooms are small only by comparison. Dine in on the night of your arrival, as the manor is rather off the beaten track. Breakfast is usually served in the pine kitchen. The Peak District is on your doorstep and the countryside is very reminiscent of Brontë country which is about an hour's drive away. *Directions:* Leave the M1 at junction 35a and take the A616 (10 miles) to Langsett. Turn right opposite the Wagon and Horses pub and, at the crossroads, turn sharp right, then go right at the Y. When you see Brockholes Lane on the left, turn right and follow the farm track for 2/3 mile.

ALDERMAN'S HEAD MANOR
Owners: Ann & Philip Unitt
Hartcliffe Hill Road
Langsett, Stocksbridge
South Yorkshire S30 5GY, England
Tel & fax: (01226) 766209
4 rooms, 3 en suite
From £22.50 per person
Closed Christmas
Children over 12
No-smoking House

Places to Stay

Treffry Farmhouse was for many years the major farm on the vast Lanhydrock estate. Now Lanhydrock is the principal National Trust property in Cornwall and Treffry Farmhouse is home to Pat and David Smith. This is very much a working farm where the cows come up the lane every morning and guests are welcome to watch the milking. There are often children around (usually in the woodland adventure playground) for the old barns in the farmyard are now lovely self-catering cottages that range from small and tidy (Granary Steps) to large and luxurious (Linhay). The farmhouse offers bed-and-breakfast accommodation in three flowery little bedrooms (Lemon, Rose, and Green), each named for the color of their decor. Guests have a pine-paneled sitting room and country-style breakfast room. A three-minute walk brings you to Lanhydrock where you get a real sense of "upstairs, downstairs" as you tour the richly furnished Victorian main rooms, maids' bedrooms, and fabulous kitchen with its enormous copper pans and old-fashioned dairy cooled by a little stream. Treffry Farmhouse is perfect for exploring Cornwall's northern (St. Ives, Tintagel, and Boscastle) and southern coasts (St. Michael's Mount, Polperro, and Mousehole). *Directions:* From Bodmin, take the B3268 towards Lostwithiel to the mini-roundabout where you turn right. The farm is on your right after 300 yards.

TREFFRY FARMHOUSE
Owners: Pat & David Smith
Lanhydrock
Bodmin
Cornwall PL30 5AF, England
Tel & fax: (01208) 74405
3 en-suite rooms
From £19 per person
Closed Christmas & New Year
Children over 6
No-smoking house

The Farmhouse Hotel and Restaurant is very much a Rouse family operation: Dad (Don) runs the dairy farm, Mum (Mary) operates the farmhouse as a hotel, son Wesley is the hotel manager, and daughter-in-law Nikki is the chef. Surrounded by its outbuildings and facing a large garden, this 17th-century Cotswold stone farmhouse has been tastefully converted while retaining the cozy charm of its walk-in fireplaces, oak beams, and low ceilings. Bedrooms are named after Oxford colleges and range from small attic rooms with dormer windows (Trinity and Keebles) to a luxurious double where the soft-pink color of the walls and carpet is picked up in the flower-sprigged drapes and ornate bedhead. Nuffield is a ground-floor room equipped for the handicapped. The restaurant has been extended from the beamed farmhouse dining room into a Victorian-style conservatory. On Friday and Saturday a more elaborate dinner menu is available while during the week a three-course meal (with choices) is offered. The Farmhouse is a very informal place: I know of no other hotel where guests can ask to visit the cows being milked. Oxford and Woodstock are just a short drive away. *Directions:* University Farm is on the A4095 (Faringdon road) 3 miles south of Witney. Unfortunately, RAF Brize Norton is nearby, so be prepared for some aircraft noise.

THE FARMHOUSE HOTEL AND RESTAURANT
Owners: The Rouse Family
University Farm, Lew
Bampton
Oxon OX18 2AU, England
Tel: (01993) 850297 Fax: (01993) 850965
6 en-suite rooms
From £25 per person
Closed Christmas & New Year
Credit cards: MC, VS
Children over 5

Tucked in an unspoiled valley high above the hustle and bustle of the more well-known Lake District tourist routes, this traditional pub lies surrounded by the ruggedly beautiful Lakeland scenery. Built of somber-looking slate in 1872 as a resting place for travelers, the hostelry is still a base for tourists, many of whom come here for the walking. They gather by the bar, the sound of their hiking boots echoing hollowly against the slate floor, poring over maps and discussing the day's activities. By contrast, the carpeted and curtained dining room and lounge with its velour chairs seem very sedate. The Stephenson family pride themselves on the quality of their food and offer a five-course meal in addition to substantial bar meals. Do not expect grand things of the accommodations as this is not a luxury establishment. However, for travelers who enjoy quietly decorated, simply furnished, and spotlessly clean rooms with modern bathrooms, the Three Shires fits the bill. Just a few miles away are some of the Lake District's most popular villages: Hawkshead, Ambleside, Coniston, and Grasmere. *Directions:* From Ambleside take the A593, Coniston road, cross Skelwith Bridge, and take the first right, signposted The Langdales and Wrynose Pass. Take the first left to Little Langdale and the Three Shires Inn is on your right.

THREE SHIRES INN
Owners: The Stephenson Family
Little Langdale
Ambleside
Cumbria LA22 9N2, England
Tel: (015394) 37215
10 en-suite rooms
From £28 per person
Closed January
Children welcome

Built in 1673 as a rectory, Landewednack House sits above the 6th-century church and a cluster of thatched cottages which lead down to the rocky inlet of Church Cove at the tip of the Lizard peninsula. Newly restored to a state of luxury unknown to former residents, Landewednack House was purchased in 1994 by Marion and Peter Stanley who fell in love with the house, its walled garden, and magnificent views. Guests are welcomed with a traditional Cornish tea of scones, clotted cream, and strawberry jam served in the elegant sitting room. In the evening guests dine together in the dining room before a log fire in the massive 17th-century fireplace. Upstairs, the large yellow bedroom's windows frame the church and the sea. The other two bedrooms are furnished with antiques and one has its Jacuzzi bathroom across the hall. This southern-most spot in England is far from the crowds. Walk along the clifftops to the adorable village of Cadgwith where you can watch the fishermen pull their boats high up the shingle beach. *Directions:* From Helston, take the A3083 to Lizard and turn left before entering the village, signposted Church Cove and Houselbay. Take the next left turn, signposted Church Cove and Lifeboat Station, and Landewednack House is on your left through the large granite gateposts.

LANDEWEDNACK HOUSE
Owners: Marion & Peter Stanley
Church Cove
Lizard
Helston
Cornwall TR12 7PQ, England
Tel: (01326) 290909 Fax: (01326) 290192
3 rooms, 2 en suite
From £25 per person
Closed Christmas
Children over 12
No-smoking house

The village of Llanmynech straddles the border between Wales and England, making it the perfect location for exploring both Shropshire and North Wales. In order to make their home more spacious, Carol and Bryan Fahey have combined two small front rooms into a guest dining and sitting room with a log fire for colder weather. The house was for many years the village Dame School and a photo of the class of 1904 hangs in the hallway. Up the narrow staircase are three attractive bedrooms (the single and twin are snug and cottagey while the double is large enough to accommodate a lovely Victorian half-tester bed). The guestrooms share a bathroom and a shower room. If visitors are staying for several days, Carol can sometimes assign private facilities. As a retired catering lecturer, Carol offers a high standard of cuisine at moderate cost, which she feels contributes to her having so many return guests. Bryan, a keen fly-fisherman, is happy to give advice and make fishing arrangements for guests. The Faheys are keen walkers, as are many of their guests who come to hike along Offa's Dyke and enjoy walking beside the Montgomery Canal. A lovely day out in Wales could include visiting Llanrhaeder waterfall and a drive around Lake Vyrnwy. *Directions:* From Oswestry, take the A483 towards Welshpool for 5½ miles to the village of Llanmynech. Turn left on the B4398 toward Knockin and after ¼ mile cross the humpback bridge: Vyrnwy Bank is the fourth house on the left.

VYRNWY BANK
Owners: Carol & Bryan Fahey
Llanmynech
Shropshire SY22 6LG, England
Tel: (01691) 830427
3 rooms, none en suite
From £15 per person
Open February to December
Children welcome

When the Richardses bought this house they were unaware that their cottage-style home with its maze of little rooms was in fact a medieval great hall with giant wooden beams and roof trusses. Careful restoration has revealed the large parlor below and the great hall above. While the parlor with its mullioned windows, beamed ceiling, and sofas arranged before the huge stone fireplace causes guests to "ooh and aah," it is the great hall that makes them gasp as they regard the massive roof trusses and the maze of intricate timberwork soaring overhead. The soft glow of flickering candlelight bathes guests as they dine at the refectory table in the great hall. Cozy, beamed bedrooms are decorated to perfection in country-print fabrics and have accompanying bathrooms neatly tucked under the rafters. The garden, which is completely encircled by a wide moat, has a willow-shaded fish pond which is home to lazily swimming ducks. Nearby Shrewsbury with its twisting lanes, castle, and open-pillared market hall deserves exploration. Farther afield are the Ironbridge Gorge Museum and the historic town of Ludlow. *Directions:* From Shrewsbury take the A49 south for 8 miles: Longnor is signposted to the left. Go through the village past the school and turn left into the lane marked "No Through Road." When the lane turns left, Moat House is straight ahead.

MOAT HOUSE
Owners: Margaret & Peter Richards
Longnor
Shrewsbury
Shropshire SY5 7PP, England
Tel & fax: (01743) 718434
2 en-suite rooms
From £35 per person
Open April to October
Credit cards: all major
Children not accepted
Wolsey Lodge

This endearing cottage dates back to the early 14th century when it was home to a yeoman farmer. With its little upstairs windows peeking out from beneath a heavy thatch roof and its timber-framed wall fronted by a flower-filled garden, Loxley Farm presents an idyllic picture. The picture-book ambiance is continued inside where guests have a tiny parlor and dine together round a long table in the low-beamed dining room. Up the broad polished stairs is a suite of rooms consisting of a sitting room, bedroom, and bathroom. With their beams, and sloping ceilings and floors these provide the premium accommodation. Across the garden a timbered building has been converted to provide more contemporary accommodation: a bedroom at either end with a living room and kitchen between. Breakfast is the only meal served and guests often walk into Loxley to dine or go to The Bell in Alderminster. A quiet back road brings you into the center of Stratford-upon-Avon, birthplace of the greatest poet in the English language, William Shakespeare. Here there are historical timbered buildings to investigate, lovely shops, and the Royal Shakespeare Theatre. In nearby Shottery is Anne Hathaway's picture-book cottage. Warwick Castle and Coventry Cathedral are both easily visited from Loxley. *Directions:* Loxley is signpost off the A422 Stratford-upon-Avon to Banbury road about 4 miles from Stratford on the left. Go through the village to the bottom of the hill, turn left (Stratford-upon-Avon), and Loxley Farm is the third house on the right.

LOXLEY FARM
Owners: Anne & Rod Hornton
Loxley
Warwickshire CV35 9JN, England
Tel: (01789) 840265
3 en-suite rooms
From £22 per person
Closed for Christmas
Children welcome

This elegant Georgian townhouse was built in 1770 and designed by Sir James Gibbs of Radcliffe Library (Oxford) and St. Martins in the Fields (Trafalgar Square) fame. Michael and Guy have decorated their home with great flair and added the most enviable collection of paintings and antique furniture. A great deal of effort is put into the evening meals. Breakfast is ordered the night before and served promptly at the time of your choosing. Stairs wind up to the sitting rooms and up again to the bedrooms (there are lots of stairs and no lift). While the principal bedroom sports a decorative, wrought-iron-and-brass bed, I preferred the adjacent spacious twin-bedded room. Farther up the house is a brass half-tester double-bedded room and another standard twin-bedded room. All these rooms overlook the walls and gardens of Ludlow Castle. If you're up to the climb, there's a sweet little bedroom under the eaves that looks south towards the river. Guests are not given door or room keys. Ludlow, its castle, marketplace, and antique and second-hand bookshops are on your doorstep. Stokesay Castle and Powys Castle and garden are great attractions as are the nearby towns of Worcester and Shrewsbury. *Directions:* Take the one-way system through Ludlow almost to the castle gates. With the walls on your right, turn left down Dinham and look for the three burgundy-colored doors. There is unrestricted parking on the street.

NUMBER ELEVEN
Owners: Guy Crawley & Michael Martin
Dinham
Ludlow
Shropshire SY8 1EJ, England
Tel: (01584) 878584
5 en-suite rooms
From £28 per person
Open all year
Children over 12
No-smoking house

The Salweys of Shropshire can trace their lineage hereabouts back to 1216 and The Lodge has been in their family since it was built in the early 1700s, but it is definitely not a formal place. Hermione puts guests at ease, encouraging them to feel as though they are friends of the family, and enjoys pointing out the architectural details of the house and explaining who's who amongst the family portraits. In the evening, guests gather in the morning room and help themselves to drinks from the honesty bar before going into dinner at a spectacular long table made of burled wood, made especially for the house. Up the grand staircase the three large bedrooms are most attractive: Chinese has a suite of furniture painted in an Asian motif, Roses is a large double with an enormous bathroom, and The Yellow Room is a large twin with its bathroom across the hall. The large garden, woodland, and farmland make this an ideal place for walking. The nearest tourist attraction is the medieval town of Ludlow with its old inns, alleyways of antique shops, Norman castle, and riverside walks. *Directions:* Leave Ludlow over Ludford Bridge traveling south. After 1½ miles turn right on the B4361 signposted Richards Castle. After 400 yards turn right through the entrance gates of The Lodge by a curved stone wall, and continue up the long drive to the house.

THE LODGE
Owners: Hermione & Humphrey Salwey
Ludlow
Shropshire SY8 4DU, England
Tel: (01584) 872103 Fax: (01584) 876126
3 rooms, 2 en suite
From £35 per person
Open April to October
Children not accepted
Wolsey Lodge

How unusual to find an outstanding Elizabethan manor amidst the suburbs and how lucky that this manor is a 15-minute drive from Heathrow airport, making it absolutely perfect for your first and last nights in England if you are visiting from overseas. Carved faces by the massive front door, bowed leaded windows, paneling, and beams make this the most impressive of homes where the warmest of welcomes is offered by Bar and her sister Sue. Relax in the oak-paneled sitting room or curl up in the upstairs hallway nook with a cup of tea and biscuits. Bedrooms are delightful: the large paneled double has an en-suite shower, the twin is decorated in sunny lemons and has its bathroom across the hall, and the small double room has a little sitting area in the tall bay window which overlooks the lovely garden. For dinner guests often walk to the pub down the road. Maidenhead railway station is only a mile away and a 30-minute train ride finds you in London—ideal for the theater or sightseeing. Windsor, Henley on Thames, and Marlow are a 15-minute drive away, while Oxford is 45 minutes away. *Directions:* Leave the M4 at junction 8/9 and take the A404 (M) to junction 9A signposted Cox Green. Follow the Cox Green signs at both mini-roundabouts into Cox Green Road. Turn left at the Foresters pub and Beehive Manor is on your right in 600 yards.

BEEHIVE MANOR
Owners: Bar Barbour & Sue Lemin
Cox Green Lane
Maidenhead
Berkshire SL6 3ET, England
Tel: (01628) 20980
3 rooms, 2 en suite
From £28 per person
Closed Christmas
Children over 12
No-smoking house

For centuries Barracott farm has been tucked in a gentle hillside overlooking Hayne Down and Hound Tor at the heart of Dartmoor. This wild and beautiful area is now a national park and Barracott the home of Val and Jim Lee. Guests enter this stone house via the Alpine garden and through a Dutch door into the broad hallway and cozy guests' sitting room where guests are served a spectacular, mouth-watering, multi-course breakfast including homemade yogurt and fresh-baked bread. From the sitting room, a doorway opens to a little staircase which leads up to the two cottage-style bedrooms, simply decorated with matching drapes and bedspreads (one bathroom en suite and one down the hall). For dinner you are directed to The Kestor in Manaton or the Rock Inn in Haytor Vale. Falling under the spell of this lovely spot, visitors often walk Easdon Moor, which rises behind Barracott, to explore its hut circles which are the ancient foundations of Bronze-Age homes. The wild beauty of Dartmoor with its sheltered villages and market towns has a magic all its own; with deep valleys, rushing streams, and wild moorlands. Buckfast and Buckland abbeys, National Trust properties such as Castle Drago, the Devonshire coast, and Cornwall are among the sightseeing possibilities. *Directions:* From Exeter take the A38 to the A382, Bovey Tracy, turnoff. At the second roundabout turn left following signs for Manaton. Go through Manaton and, beyond the village, turn left at the T-junction and then take the first right to Barracott.

BARRACOTT
Owners: Val & Jim Lee
Manaton
Newton Abbot
Devon TQ13 9XA, England
Tel: (01647) 221312
2 rooms, 1 en suite
From £22.50 per person
Open April to October
Children welcome if family takes both rooms

Conjecture has it that Thomas Hardy used Old Lamb House (then the Lamb Inn) as Rollivers Tavern in *Tess of the d'Urbervilles*. Jenny and Ben continue the tradition of hospitality by offering accommodation to guests in two large front bedrooms which share a bathroom. Guests use the front door (while family use the kitchen door) and atop the curving staircase there's a sitting area with two armchairs and lots of tourist information. Jenny finds that most guests prefer to relax in their bedrooms, both of which contain comfortable, old-fashioned armchairs. The Pink Room is decked out in soft pinks with matching flowery bed-linen and drapes, while the Gray Room is outfitted in soft blue-grays and offers lovely views of the garden with its stately cedar tree. Guests usually drive the short distance to the Crown or the Blackmore Vale pubs for dinner. Restaurant-goers are directed to Jesters in Shaftesbury. Dorset abounds in country lanes that lead to pretty villages such as Milton Abbas and Cerne Abbas with its club-wielding giant carved into the chalk hillside. Shaftesbury has many steep roads running down into Blackmore Vale, the most famous being cobbled Gold Hill. *Directions:* From Shaftesbury take the A30 towards Exeter for 4 miles to East Stour. Turn left on B3092 to Marnhull (3 miles) and go half a mile beyond Marnhull church where you turn right at the triangle of grass with a signpost and into Old Lamb House's driveway.

OLD LAMB HOUSE
Owners: Jenny & Ben Chilcott
Marnhull
Dorset DT10 1QG, England
Tel: (01258) 820491 Fax: (01258) 821464
2 rooms, none en suite
From £17 per person
Closed Christmas
Children welcome
No-smoking house

Middleham is an attractive town of gray-stone houses sitting beneath the ruins of Middleham Castle. Separated from the cobbled market square by a rose garden, Waterford House is much older than its Victorian exterior suggests. Built as a substantial family home, the house was in recent times divided into two by a husband and wife who wished to live apart but remain in the same village. Now, happily, it is a single house again and the only reminder of its days as two homes are the stairways at either side of the house that lead to the bedrooms. These delightful bedrooms are furnished, as is the entire house, with lovely old furniture and Everyl and Brian's collections of all things old and interesting. A large double room has an extra bed and families with two children appreciate the bunk beds tucked neatly into the corner of the largest bedroom (the only room with a bathroom across the hall). An integral part of your stay here is sampling the delicious dinners that Everyl prepares and serves in the antique-packed dining room. The dinner menu changes slightly every night and completely every week and you can dine à la carte or choose an evening-long five-course dinner. Waterford House is an ideal central location for exploring the Yorkshire dales. *Directions:* Leave the A1 on the B6267 to Masham and on to Middleham. Waterford House is on your left (on the Leyburn road) just beyond the town's cobbled square.

WATERFORD HOUSE **NEW**
Owners: Everyl & Brian Madell
19 Kirkgate
Middleham
North Yorkshire DL8 4PG, England
Tel & fax: (01969) 622090 or Fax: (01969) 624020
5 rooms, 4 en suite
From £30 per person
Open all year
Credit cards: MC, VS
Children welcome

Mungrisdale is one of the few unspoilt villages left in the Lake District and is made up of a pub, an old church, and a cluster of houses and farms set at the foot of rugged, gray-blue crags. Do not confuse The Mill with the adjoining pub, The Mill Inn: drive through car park of the inn to reach private parking for this cozy hotel. Rooms are of cottage proportions: a small lounge with comfy chairs gathered round a blazing log fire, a cozy dining room where each small oak table is set with blue napkins, candles, willow-pattern china, and a tiny flower arrangement, and nine small bedrooms with matching draperies and bedspreads. Most visitors are drawn here for the outstanding dinners prepared by Eleanor. Dinner consists of an appetizer followed by a tasty homemade soup served with soda bread (the latter a popular fixture on the menu), a main course (with a vegetarian alternative), dessert, and cheese and biscuits. Bookings for bed and breakfast only are not usually accepted. The Lake District is a beautiful region, popular with walkers and sightseers alike. Some of its premier villages are Coniston, Hawkshead, Sawrey (home of Beatrix Potter), Ambleside, and Grasmere. *Directions:* Leave the M6 at junction 40 and take the A66 towards Keswick for 10 miles. The Mill is 2 miles north of this road and the signpost for Mungrisdale is midway between Penrith and Keswick.

THE MILL HOTEL
Owners: Eleanor & Richard Quinlan
Mungrisdale
Penrith
Cumbria CA11 0XR, England
Tel: (017687) 79659
9 rooms, 7 en suite
From £48 per person dinner, bed & breakfast
Open February to November
Children welcome

In her younger years Beatrix Potter used to visit Ees Wyke House with her family. Now it is a very pleasant hotel run by Mag and John Williams who have painted and decorated the house from top to bottom in a comfortable style. They are constantly improving the standards at their hotel, the latest project being the addition of a large dining room with glorious views across the countryside. John, a former cookery teacher at a catering college, enjoys cooking. His dinner menu always offers choices of starter, main courses, and desserts. The bedrooms have tall windows framing gorgeous countryside views and many overlook nearby Esthwaite Water. Tucked under the eaves, two airy, spacious attic bedrooms have super views: one has a bathroom en suite while the other has a private bath just next door. The other bedrooms also have a mix of en-suite and adjacent bathroom arrangements. The smallest bedroom, on the ground floor, is reserved for visitors who have difficulty with stairs but unfortunately has no view. A short stroll up the village brings you to Hill Top Farm where Beatrix Potter wrote several of her books. Walks abound in the area and the more oft-trod Lakeland routes are easily accessible by taking the nearby ferry across Lake Windermere. *Directions:* From Ambleside take the A593 towards Coniston. After about a mile turn left on the B5286 to Hawkshead. Skirt Hawkshead village and follow signs for the ferry. Ees Wyke House is on the right just before Sawrey.

EES WYKE COUNTRY HOUSE HOTEL
Owners: Mag & John Williams
Near Sawrey
Hawkshead, Ambleside
Cumbria LA22 0JZ, England
Tel: (015394) 36393
8 rooms, 6 en suite
From £36 per person
Closed January
Children over 10 & babies

The quiet, narrow country lane that runs in front of Fosse Farmhouse is the historical Fosse Way, the road built by the Romans to connect their most important forts from Devon to Lincolnshire. Caron Cooper has furnished her rooms with great flair using soft colors and enviable country-French antiques in every room. Charming collectibles and country china adorn much of the sitting and breakfast rooms and most pieces are for sale. Upstairs there are three extremely comfortable guest bedrooms. My favorite was The Pine Room with its mellow pine furniture and especially spacious, luxuriously equipped bathroom. Across the courtyard, the ground floor of the stables has been converted to a tea room and restaurant. On the floor above, three cottage-style bedrooms are stylishly decorated in white on white. With advance notice, Caron enjoys preparing an imaginative, three-course dinner, and is happy to cater to vegetarian palates. At Christmas time Caron offers a three-day festive holiday. This tranquil countryside setting is within an easy half-hour's drive of Bath, Bristol, Tetbury, and Cirencester and the picture-perfect village of Castle Combe is also nearby. *Directions:* Exit the M4 at junction 17 towards Chippenham, turn right on the A420 (Bristol road) for 3 miles to the B4039 which you take around Castle Combe to The Gib where you turn left opposite The Salutation Inn. Fosse Farmhouse is on your right after 1 mile.

FOSSE FARMHOUSE
Owner: Caron Cooper
Nettleton Shrub, Nettleton
Chippenham
Wiltshire SN14 7NJ, England
Tel: (01249) 782286 Fax: (01249) 783066
6 en-suite rooms
From £40 per person
Open all year
Credit cards: all major
Children welcome

Set in the picturesque moorland village of North Bovey, frequent winner of the best-kept Dartmoor village award, Gate House has a lovely location just behind the tree-lined village green. The location and warm welcome offered by hosts Sheila and John Williams add up to the perfect recipe for a countryside holiday. The sitting room has an ancient bread oven tucked inside a massive granite fireplace beneath a low beamed ceiling, and the adjacent dining room has a pine table in front of an atmospheric old stove. A narrow stairway leads up from the dining room to two of the guest bedrooms, each with a neat bathroom tucked under the eaves. The third bedroom is found at the top of another little staircase, this one off the sitting room, and affords views through a huge copper beech to the swimming pool (unheated) which guests are welcome to use, and idyllic green countryside. Sheila prepares a lovely country breakfast and a four-course evening meal (including vegetarian dishes if requested). Apart from walking on the moor and touring the moorland villages, many guests enjoy golf at the nearby Manor Hotel. The Devon coastline is easily accessible and many guests take a day trip into Cornwall, often venturing as far afield as Clovelly. *Directions:* From Exeter take the A38 to the A382, Bovey Tracy, turnoff. Turn left in Mortenhampstead onto the Princetown road, then immediately left again to North Bovey, go down the lane into the village and Gate House is on the left beyond the Ring of Bells.

GATE HOUSE
Owners: Sheila & John Williams
North Bovey
Devon TQ13 8RB, England
Tel & fax: (01647) 440479
3 en-suite rooms
From £24 per person
Closed Christmas & February
Children over 15

Rectory Farm was purchased by Robert's grandparents in 1915. While Robert continues the family farming tradition, his wife Mary Anne offers bed-and-breakfast accommodation in their lovely Elizabethan farmhouse. Mary Anne and Robert have put a lot of effort into tastefully modernizing and refurbishing their very old home. Guests have a small sitting and breakfast room with a woodburning stove. Upstairs, a modern shower room has been added to the large twin-bedded room where you sleep beneath an unusual ceiling whose support beam is covered in decorative plasterwork. A lovely fireplace was unearthed in this room during remodeling. A smaller pine double bedroom has an en-suite shower room and sits among the family's bedrooms. Breakfast is the only meal served, so guests often enjoy dinner at the Red Lion pub in the village or the Harcourt Arms in nearby Stanton Harcourt. The farmlands border the River Thames where you can walk along the towpath and go fishing. An hour's drive will find you in Stratford-upon-Avon or Bath. Closer at hand, you can tour the Oxford colleges, try your hand at punting, and visit Blenheim Palace where Churchill was born. *Directions:* From Oxford, take the A420 (Swindon) to Kingston Bagpuize, turn right on the A415 (Witney), cross the river and turn immediately right beside the Rose Revived car park. After 2 miles turn right at the T-junction, and Rectory Farm is on the right beside the church.

RECTORY FARM
Owners: Mary Anne & Robert Florey
Northmoor
Witney
Oxfordshire OX8 1SX, England
Tel: (01865) 300207
2 en-suite rooms
From £20 per person
Open February to mid-December
Children over 14
No-smoking house

The Grange, a former rectory, is a rambling Regency home covered with wisteria, comfortably furnished by Sue and Malcolm Whittley. Guests are welcome to use the cozy television room or the formal drawing room overlooking the vast expanses of sweeping lawn and mature trees. The four bedrooms range in size from a large twin room softly carpeted in pink with light-pink walls and cushioned window seats, to a compact double room with sunny yellow walls prettily furnished in country pine. Homey touches such as hanging bouquets of dried flowers, pictures on the walls, and even a Paddington bear on a corner shelf add warmth. Amidst the 5 acres of lawns and gardens, tucked behind the kitchen garden and beyond the ducks and peacocks, is a walled swimming pool. Northwold is within easy reach of Norwich with its splendid castle museum and cathedral, the ancient university town of Cambridge, the medieval market town of King's Lynn, and the unspoilt, scenic North Norfolk coast. Nearby are the Royal Family's summer home, Sandringham House, the Caley Mill lavender farm, and the church in Heacham where John Rolfe married his Indian princess, Pocohontas. *Directions:* From King's Lynn take the A134, signposted Thetford, to Northwold. Turn left into the village, pass the church and the Old Rectory (on the left), and turn left in front of the row of cottages which brings you into The Grange's driveway.

THE GRANGE
Owners: Sue & Malcolm Whittley
Northwold
Thetford
Norfolk IP26 5NF, England
Tel: (01366) 728240
4 rooms, 2 en suite
From £18 per person
Closed Christmas
Children over 5

While The Plaine is the name of this guesthouse, it also is the name of the area of the village that was used for centuries as the market place. Sadly, the days of markets are long gone and the market cross has been dismantled so that large trucks can negotiate the village streets. Fortunately, evenings are quiet and you can enjoy the village's lovely old buildings. Guests have a snug sitting room and dine together round the long dining-room table where breakfast is the only meal served. For dinner The George and the Fleur de Lys serve good food in atmospheric pubs dating back to medieval times. One bedroom is on the ground floor, while the other two are found up a circular stone staircase. The bedrooms are all about the same size and have reproduction four-poster beds draped in flowery fabrics that coordinate with the curtains. Norton St. Philip is an ideal location for visiting Georgian Bath with its wealth of attractions and Wells with its magnificent cathedral set in spacious grounds. During the quiet evening hours you can follow a walking tour that leads you round the village. *Directions:* From Bath take the A367 (Exeter road) and at the end of the dual carriageway turn left on the B3110 signposted Frome. Go through the villages of Midford and Hinton Charthouse to Norton St. Philip where you find The Plaine on your left opposite The George pub.

THE PLAINE GUEST HOUSE
Owners: Gill & Terry Gazzard
Norton St. Philip
Bath
Avon BA3 6LE, England
Tel: (01373) 834723 Fax: (01373) 834101
3 en-suite rooms
From £23.50 per person
Open all year
Credit cards: all major
Children welcome
No-smoking house

The river estuaries around Plymouth provide sheltered harbors for sailboats. Bobbing yachts fill the inlets, narrow lanes wind around wooded headlands, and the shores are lined with pretty, pastel-washed homes. Rowan Cottage has been Jeannie's home for many years and she has turned what was a pocket-sized home into a spacious habitation. The large double-bedded room's ceiling rises to the rafters and has a door in the bathroom that leads into the flower-filled garden. A snug single room, all decked out in blue and white, has its bathroom across the hall. Jeannie and Guy are very casual, very warm hosts who join their guests for dinner and conversation, settling them afterwards with coffee and chocolates in the large beamed sitting room with its views across the estuary. If guests prefer, they will direct them to local pubs and restaurants which serve excellent food. The Hollebones can arrange to take you sailing on their 32-foot Moody. Famous voyagers, such as the Pilgrim Fathers and Captain Cook, who set out on historic journeys are commemorated in nearby Plymouth. *Directions:* Leave the A38 (Exeter to Plymouth road) at the sign to Yealmpton and Ugborough. Continue to Yealmpton and take a left fork to Noss Mayo (3½ miles). Keep the river on your right all the way to Bridgend Quay, and Rowan Cottage is the first cottage on your left, up the lane.

ROWAN COTTAGE
Owners: Jeannie & Guy Hollebone
Bridgend, Noss Mayo
Plymouth
Devon PL8 1DX, England
Tel: (01752) 872714
2 rooms, 1 en suite
From £29 per person
Closed for Christmas
Children over 12
No-smoking house
Wolsey Lodge

Jane and Robin Halfhead take only one party of guests at a time in their lovely home because Jane feels it is important that guests not share a bathroom with people they do not know. The two very pretty guestrooms consist of a twin-bedded room and an airy room where the twin beds can be zipped together to make a king-sized bed. In the morning, guests enjoy breakfast in front of the Aga at a country-pine table beneath the kitchen beam decorated with dried hops. In the evening, Jane and Robin join their guests for a drink before dinner and dine with them round the dining-room table. The tariff for dinner includes wine and a pre-dinner drink. Beyond the lovely house the garden opens up to miles of very gently rolling countryside. Guests are welcome to use the tennis court or enjoy a game of croquet on the lawn. Oaksey is on the southernmost edge of the Cotswolds and guests often visit the old market towns of Tetbury and Malmesbury with their lovely buildings and attractive shops. Farther afield lie Bath and Cheltenham. *Directions:* From Cirencester, take the A429 towards Malmesbury for 6½ miles, passing through Kemble, and turn left at the crossroads for the 2-mile drive to Oaksey. Go through the village and Oaksey Court is the second-to-last house on the right.

OAKSEY COURT
Owners: Jane & Robin Halfhead
Oaksey
Malmesbury
Wiltshire SN16 9TF, England
Tel: (01666) 577265
2 rooms, none en suite
From £25 per person
Closed Christmas & New Year
Children over 10
No-smoking house
Wolsey Lodge

Lise and Michael Hilton have done the most magnificent job of converting a 17th-century barn and stable into an exquisite home. Huge timbers reach to the apex of the hayloft in the living room where high-backed sofas are drawn cozily round the fire, a baby grand piano occupies an alcove and the room opens up to a vast billiard room that the Hiltons encourage guests to enjoy. Lovely pictures and plate collections adorn the walls, and enviable antiques furnish every nook and cranny. A lovely four-poster bedroom is found up the main staircase while across the courtyard two lovely bedrooms occupy the restored carriage house. Lise and Michael are the most gracious of hosts and enjoy helping guests plan their sightseeing and dining. If you are staying during the week, be sure to make a reservation for one of Lise's delicious dinners (bring your own wine to accompany the meal). Unspoiled Suffolk villages are close at hand, Constable country is within easy reach as are Dunwich, the medieval village that has almost been claimed by the sea, the elegant seaside resort of Southwold, Minsmere Bird Reserve, and the concert hall at Snape. Sample local wines at the Bruisyard St. Peter winery in the village of Bruisyard—you may come away with a case. *Directions:* Otley is 6 miles northeast of Ipswich. With the post office on your right, Bowerfield is on your right after a quarter of a mile. Lise will send or fax you detailed driving instructions.

BOWERFIELD HOUSE
Owners: Lise & Michael Hilton
Otley
Ipswich
Suffolk IP6 9NR, England
Tel: (01473) 890742 Fax: (01473) 890059
3 en-suite rooms
From £21 per person
Open March to November
Children over 12

The charm of Anne and Jim O'Kane and the sparkling condition of this modern suburban home just 2 miles from the historic heart of Oxford won me over completely. Jim, with his soft Irish lilt, and Anne offer a genuine warmth of welcome and never tire of poring over maps with guests to point them in the right direction for enjoying this wonderful historic city. Everything about their bedrooms is of the highest standards: each is equipped with either a double, twin, or a double and twin beds, and shower room and is kitted out with a small refrigerator, tea and coffee tray, biscuits, chocolates, wine glasses—everything you need to make you feel at home. I was particularly impressed by the spacious ground-floor double room (room 7) and rooms 5 and 1 which contain both a double and a single bed. Jim is especially proud that Cotswold House is included in an Inspector Morse detective book. A hearty traditional English or vegetarian breakfast are the only meals served. For dinner guests are directed to a local pub, The Kings, or the popular Brown's restaurant in the center of town. Leave your car in the forecourt and take the bus into town. Jim suggests that your first port of call be the Oxford Tourist Office where the informative two-hour walking tours start from. *Directions:* Cotswold House is on the left, on the A4206, Banbury Road, 2 miles from the center of Oxford.

COTSWOLD HOUSE **NEW**
Owners: Anne & Jim O'Kane
363 Banbury Road
Oxford OX2 7PL, England
Tel & fax: (01865) 310558
7 en-suite rooms
From £27 per person
Open all year
Children over 5
No-smoking house

Jean and Jack Langton are the most delightful, attentive hosts and Jean is an accomplished cook who always offers her guests a splendid dinner, or, if they prefer a less substantial meal, supper. Jean and Jack dine with their guests around the prettily set dining-room table which overlooks their large back garden. Set in a charming countryside village, The Old Rectory began life as two tiny cottages, home to the vicar's coachman and the butler. At the turn of the century the cottages were combined and became the vicarage. Parkham's vicars liked to change residences—there are three old rectories in the village. The Langtons' home is decorated in a light, airy way and while it does not abound in antiques, there is a traditional feel to the house. The largest double bedroom overlooks the garden as does a smaller double room which has its private bathroom across the hall. Guests seek out Jean in the kitchen and chat around the Aga planning their sightseeing excursions which invariably include the Royal Horticultural Society gardens, Rosemoor in Torrington, and Marwood Hill with its national collection of astibes. Clovelly, the famous, somewhat over-commercialized village, is a great attraction, as is the Dartington glass factory in Torrington. *Directions:* From Bideford take the A39 south to Horns Cross (Coach and Horses inn) and turn left for Parkham. Turn left by the church and left at the second turning on the right. At The Bell pub turn left and The Old Rectory is on your right halfway down the hill.

THE OLD RECTORY
Owners: Jean & Jack Langton
Parkham Nr Bideford
Devon EX39 5PL, England
Tel: (01237) 451443
3 rooms, 2 en suite
From £35 per person
Closed Christmas
Children over 12
No-smoking house

Penryn is a very much a working town whose main thoroughfare, Broad Street, runs up the hill from the fishing quay. Halfway up the hill, fronting directly onto the street, you find Clare House. Built in the 17th century as an impressive gentleman's residence, it was restored several years ago by Jean and Jack Hewitt who ran the town's newsagents for many years. Jean is chatty and friendly and, while guests have their own spacious sitting room, she often whisks them to her side of the house where she and Jack join them for tea and a chat in their sitting room or in the Victorian conservatory with its hundred-year-old grapevine. Jean finds that having bed-and-breakfast guests has expanded her circle of friends from the town to the world. Bedrooms at the front of the house are particularly large: one has its shower cubicle and sink in the room and the loo across the hall while the other has its private bathroom across the hall. The third bedroom is quietly located at the back of the house and has en-suite facilities. A small refreshment room stocked with tea, coffee, soft drinks, and biscuits is located between the bedrooms. Guests often walk to the Waterfront restaurant or drive to the Pandora, an adorable, thatched inn overlooking Restronguet Creek. *Directions:* From Truro, take the A39 toward Falmouth. Follow the second signpost to Penryn and turn right at the traffic lights on the quay into Broad Street—Clare House is on the left.

CLARE HOUSE
Owners: Jean & Jack Hewitt
20 Broad Street
Penryn
Cornwall TR10 8JH, England
Tel: (01326) 373294
3 rooms, 1 en suite
From £22 per person
Closed Christmas & New Year
Children over 12
No-smoking house

While Prospect House's location is commercial (it's next to a telephone exchange and opposite a car showroom), the house is set back from the main road and enjoys a large garden. The lane that runs beside it meanders past fishermen's cottages to the main street of Penryn which climbs the hill from the harbor to the unusual long, narrow town hall which sits in the middle of the road. Cliff and Barry forsook their careers in teaching and theater management to run this attractive guesthouse. The comfortable sitting room has an intricate plasterwork frieze bordering the ceiling while the dining room, which was at one time the kitchen, retains its large fireplace and uneven flagstone floor. Barry and Cliff commissioned a handsome dining-room table to match the delicate Flemish dining chairs. The three bedrooms are named after clipper ships that sailed from Penryn harbor. Waterwitch, the most spacious bedroom, overlooks the pretty garden and has a large bathroom. On the landing there is a refreshment area where you can make tea and coffee or select juices, soft drinks, and ice from the refrigerator. Cornwall has an abundance of secluded river estuaries (Helford estuary was Daphne du Maurier's Frenchman's Creek), an abundance of gardens (Trelissick, Glendurgan, Trebah), and friendly villages down switchback lanes. *Directions:* From Truro take the A39 towards Falmouth, then the B3292. Ignore the first signpost into Penryn—Prospect House is on the corner opposite the Volvo dealership.

PROSPECT HOUSE
Owners: Barry Sheppard & Cliff Paul
1 Church Road
Penryn
Cornwall TR10 8DA, England
Tel & fax: (01326) 373198
3 en-suite rooms
From £23.50 per person
Open all year
Children over 12

Swale Cottage is down a tiny country lane on the outskirts of Penshurst. Here Cynthia Dakin spent a year converting an 18th-century barn into a pretty home. Everything is cottage-cozy with white-painted walls and black beams. Cynthia's paintings (many of them of local scenery) decorate the walls. Breakfast is the only meal served on the oak refectory table and guests often go to the George and Dragon in Speldhurst (reputedly one of England's oldest pubs) or the Castle Inn in the pretty village of Chiddingstone. Upstairs, the bedrooms are cottagey in their decor and, while the four-poster is the largest room, I preferred the smaller double with its brass-and-iron bedstead and small bathroom. A twin bedroom has its bathroom across the hall. Guests enjoy a walk across the fields to Penshurst Place with its magnificent Tudor garden. It's a ten-minute drive to Hever Castle (Anne Boleyn's childhood home) and Chartwell (Churchill's home). The information packet in the rooms contains a useful chart which outlines the prices, times, and days of opening of the most popular 20 houses, castles, and gardens in the area. *Directions:* From Tunbridge Wells take the A26 north for 2½ miles and turn left onto the B2176 to Penshurst (3 miles). Half a mile before reaching Penshurst turn left into Poundsbridge Lane and, after 100 yards, right into a narrow lane signposted Swale Cottage.

SWALE COTTAGE
Owner: Cynthia Dakin
Old Swaylands Lane
off Poundsbridge Lane
Penshurst
Kent TN11 8AH, England
Tel: (01892) 870738
3 rooms, 2 en suite
From £25 per person
Open all year
Children over 10
No-smoking house

There was a farm on this site recorded in the Domesday book of 1086, though the present farm and its outbuildings date from the 1500s. Anthony's family have farmed here for generations and, while he concentrates on all things farming, Lynne concentrates on the upscale bed and breakfast that she runs in a wing of the farmhouse and the converted barns. Her accommodation is not your typical farmhousey-style: the rooms I saw were furnished with pastel-painted furniture coordinating with the draperies and bedspreads, giving a light, airy feel. Bathrooms and shower rooms are sparklingly modern and one sports a claw-foot tub and separate shower. Lynne loves to eat out and enjoys discussing dining plans with guests. She also has a folder on restaurants and traditional pubs in the area. Lynne directed us to Tencreek Farm for a scrumptious Cornish cream tea in the prettiest of gardens. If you are planning on staying for a week, consider renting the adorable little cottage for two overlooking the cow pasture. Decorated in vibrant Mediterranean colors, the cottage is excellently equipped for a romantic getaway. The idyllically pretty seaside villages of Fowey, Looe, and Polperro are great attractions as are the National Trust houses of Cotehele and Lanhydrock. *Directions:* From Looe take the A387 signposted Polperro. Before you reach Polperro, Trenderway Farm is signposted to your right.

TRENDERWAY FARM
Owners: Lynne & Anthony Tuckett
Pelynt
Polperro
Cornwall PL13 2LY, England
Tel: (01503) 72214
4 en-suite rooms
From £26 per person
Open all year
Children not accepted
No-smoking house

A humorous, tongue-in-cheek "rule" book is found in every bedroom at Bales Mead and woe betide you if you do not comply! The illustrations are drawn by Peter Clover who, with his partner Stephen Blue, runs a very tight ship in their exceptionally attractive home. Guests enjoy a sophisticated sitting room complete with log-burning fireplace and baby grand piano. Upstairs, the bedrooms are named after villages in the Porlock vale. Selworthy is cool in lemon and blue with outstanding ocean views. Bossington is all in pink, white, and mulberry with a view of the shingle beach and distant headland. Both Selworthy and Bossington have their own private bathrooms. Allerford (a smaller room overlooking the garden and woodlands) is used in conjunction with one of the other rooms by larger parties who do not mind sharing a bathroom. Breakfast is the only meal served (promptly at 9 am)—Stephen and Peter recommend excellent local pubs and restaurants for dinner. In the '50s the house was owned by a well-known horticulturist who filled the garden with specimen plants from all over the world. Just across the lane are vast stretches of shingle beach. Bales Mead is in the hamlet of West Porlock between the pretty village of Porlock and the picturesque harbor of Porlock Weir. Rising behind the house are the vast expanses of Exmoor. *Directions:* From Minehead take the A39 to Porlock, then a right turn to Porlock Weir takes you a short distance to West Porlock, where you find Bales Mead on the left.

BALES MEAD
Owners: Stephen Blue & Peter Clover
West Porlock
Somerset TA24 8NX, England
Tel: (01643) 862565
3 rooms, none en suite
From £23 per person
Closed Christmas & New Year
Children not accepted
No-smoking house

The lifeboatman has been known to deliver guests, and their luggage, to Fortitude Cottage when there's an especially high tide. While this is an adventure for visitors, Carol takes the sea coming up the road as a natural part of living beside the harbor in Old Portsmouth. When she suspects the sea may be paying a visit she simply removes the rugs from the tile floor in the little downstairs bedroom and mops the floor when the tide ebbs. This attractive room is decorated in pink candy stripes and has a small en-suite shower room. Curl up on the window seat in the airy upstairs sitting room and watch the Isle of Wight ferries and the fishing boats come and go. On the top floor two small pretty bedrooms have tiny en-suite shower rooms (request the front room with its harbor view). For dinner, Carol makes suggestions on the pubs and restaurants that are within walking distance. Take the waterbus (Easter to November) across the harbor to tour Nelson's flagship, *HMS Victory*, Henry VIII's ship, *Mary Rose*, and *HMS Warrior,* an 1861 iron-clad battleship, then go on to the submarine museum. *Directions:* Exit the M27 at junction 12, signposted Portsmouth and ferries. Follow signs for the Isle of Wight car ferry through the center of the town, then look for a brown signpost (at a roundabout) to the cathedral and Old Portsmouth. Pass the cathedral and at the end of the road turn right. Fortitude Cottage is on your left.

FORTITUDE COTTAGE
Owner: Carol Harbeck
51 Broad Street
Old Portsmouth
Hampshire PO1 2JD, England
Tel: (01705) 823748 Fax: (01705) 823748
3 en-suite rooms
From £21 per person
Closed Christmas
Credit cards: MC, VS
Children over 16

A narrow country road runs through Nidderdale (one of Yorkshire's quietest and most attractive dales) to Ramsgill, a village of a few stone houses. The Yorke Arms is tucked next to the village green with the dale rising through stone-walled fields to the high moorlands. The hotel is full of old-world charm with its polished stone flag hallway, snug little bar, traditional residents' lounge, and large restaurant with high-backed Windsor chairs and enormous dresser decorated with pewter and china. Bedrooms are spacious and each is accompanied by a sparkling bathroom or shower room. The two superior rooms are huge in size and sport comfortable seating areas and extra-large bathrooms. A good value for money is the package that includes dinner, bed, and breakfast (two or more nights). You can take beautiful walks from the hotel which vary in length from strolls by the nearby reservoir to day-long hikes over the moorlands. The ruin of Fountains Abbey, founded by Cistertian monks in 1132 and dissolved by Henry VIII, is an awesome sight and walking paths abound. A magnificent drive takes you from Grassington through Littondale to Malham Cove (one of Yorkshire's most celebrated natural features) and back to Grassington. Nearby Harrogate is an 18th-century spa town. *Directions:* From Ripon take the B6285 to Pateley Bridge where you turn right at the signpost for Ramsgill. Ramsgill is the first village after the reservoir.

THE YORKE ARMS
Managers: Kay & Colin MacDougall
Ramsgill by Harrogate
North Yorkshire HG3 5RL, England
Tel & fax: (01423) 755243
13 en-suite rooms
From £34.50 per person
Open all year
Credit cards: MC, VS
Children welcome

The Burgoyne family were people of substance hereabouts for they secured the premier building site in this picturesque Swaledale village and built an impressive home that dwarfs the surrounding buildings. Gone are the days when one family could justify such a large home and now it's a welcoming hotel run by Derek Hickson and Peter Carwardine. Derek makes guests feel thoroughly at home while Peter makes certain that they live up to their motto "'Tis substantial happiness to eat." Peter prepares a fixed-price, four-course meal every evening with plenty of choices for each course. The handsome lounge is warmed by a log fire in winter and full of inviting books on the area. There's abundant scope for walking and driving in this rugged area using Reeth as your base, though you'll be hard pressed to find a lovelier dales view than that from your bedroom window of stone-walled fields rising to vast moorlands (one bedroom faces the back of the house). Redmire and Marrick, being more spacious, are the premier rooms. Robes and slippers are provided for the occupants of Keld and Thwaite who have to slip across the hall to their bathrooms. Richmond with its medieval castle and the Bowes Museum, near Barnard Castle, with its fine collection of French furniture and porcelain, are added attractions. *Directions:* From Richmond take the A6108 towards Leyburn for 5 miles to the B6270 for the 5-mile drive to Reeth. The Burgoyne Hotel is on the village green.

THE BURGOYNE HOTEL
Owners: Derek Hickson & Peter Carwardine
Reeth
North Yorkshire DL11 6SN, England
Tel & fax: (01748) 884292
9 rooms, 6 en suite
From £30 per person
Closed January
Credit cards: MC, VS
Children welcome

Until 1990, Shawswell was a working farm in a sheltered valley beyond the little village of Rendcomb. Now it is a countryside retreat where the only sounds you hear are birdsong and the bleating of sheep which graze in the fields beyond the garden. Muriel and David Gomm have done a lovely job of keeping all the cottagey aspects of the farmhouse—the old kitchen stove in what is now the dining room, the farmhouse latch doors, and the beamed ceilings and walls. Sofas and chairs are drawn round the fire in the sitting room and it is here that David serves drinks in the evening. Breakfast is the only meal served. Upstairs, uneven corridors lead to the bedrooms where you can choose from a snug single, a twin with a huge bathroom, or a spacious four-poster Jacobean room. A 3-mile walk will find you at the Roman villa of Chedworth or the villages of Withington or Colesbourne. Within an hour's car journey are the interesting towns of Bath, Cheltenham, Gloucester, Stratford-upon-Avon, and Oxford. *Directions:* From Cirencester, take the A435 towards Cheltenham for 5 miles and turn right into the village of Rendcomb. Keep on this road (which becomes a single-track lane as it leaves the village) for 1½ miles and you come to Shawswell Country House (do not turn off the tarmac).

SHAWSWELL COUNTRY HOUSE
Owners: Muriel & David Gomm
Rendcomb
Cirencester
Gloucestershire GL7 7HD, England
Tel: (01285) 831779
5 en-suite rooms
From £22.50 per person
Open February to November
Children over 10

Whashton Springs Farm is a perfect base for exploring the Yorkshire Dales. A five-minute drive finds you at the foot of Swaledale in Richmond, with its cobbled market square and Norman castle perched high above the river. The farm is run by Gordon Turnbull and his two sons who grow corn and potatoes and run a herd of hill cows and sheep. Spring is an especially good time to visit, for the little lambs are kept close to the farm. Fairlie welcomes guests to the farmhouse and offers accommodation within the large sturdy house or in one of the delightfully private bedrooms that open directly onto the courtyard. A wing of the barn has been converted into a most attractive self-catering cottage for families who want to stay for a week. A Yorkshire farmhouse breakfast and very reasonably priced dinners are served in the dining room. Gordon serves the dinners, which gives you an opportunity to ask questions about the farm. On Sunday evenings guests are directed to local pubs and restaurants in Richmond for dinner. Within an hour you can be in Durham, York, or the Lake District. The Yorkshire Dales are on your doorstep and the North Yorkshire Moors just a half hour distant. *Directions:* From the A1, take the A6136 to Richmond. Turn right at the traffic lights signposted for Ravensworth and follow this road for 3 miles to the farm which is on your left at the bottom of a steep hill.

WHASHTON SPRINGS FARM
Owners: Fairlie & Gordon Turnbull
Richmond
North Yorkshire DL11 7JS, England
Tel: (01748) 822884
8 en-suite rooms
From £21 per person
Open February to mid-December
Children over 5

Few English guesthouses offer the ambiance, warmth, and welcome of Mizzards Farm, a lovely 16th-century farmhouse built of stone and brick. The setting is peaceful: the River Rother flows through the 13 acres of gardens and fields and the driveway winds through the large meadow-like front lawn past a small lake. The heart of the house, where breakfast is served, is especially inviting, with one wall filled by a massive inglenook fireplace and a staircase leading up to an open minstrels' gallery. In a newer wing, a sophisticated lounge is nicely furnished with antiques and highlighted by a grand piano. Twice a year concerts are held here. The home was previously owned by an English rock star who converted the largest bedroom into a glitzy, but fun, theatrical showplace with electric curtains operated from the bed on a grand dais and a marble bathroom featuring a double bathtub. The other two guestrooms are smaller and are pleasantly decorated in more traditional decor. Dinner is not served but there are many excellent choices of places to eat nearby. For the athletically minded, Mizzards also has a covered swimming pool for guests' use. *Directions:* From Petersfield take the A272 towards Midhurst. Turn right at the crossroads in Rogate, follow the road for half a mile, cross the narrow bridge over the river, and take the first right on the small lane up to Mizzards Farm.

MIZZARDS FARM
Owners: Harriet & Julian Francis
Rogate
Petersfield
Hampshire GU31 5HS, England
Tel: (01730) 821656 Fax: (01730) 821655
3 en-suite rooms
From £24 per person
Closed Christmas
Children over 6
No-smoking house

With a backdrop of mountain peaks and a lush green lawn sweeping down towards Rosthwaite village, the Hazel Bank hotel has a superb location in Borrowdale, one of the loveliest and quietest Lake District valleys. The owners, Gwen and John Nuttall, have renovated this large Victorian residence, adding modern conveniences such as sparkling bathrooms to the bedrooms to create a small comfortable hotel, all the while keeping the house's period charm and character. All the rooms are light, airy, and uncluttered. The bedrooms are named after nearby mountains. The largest rooms are Scafell Pike, a twin-bedded room that overlooks the beginning of the Scafell range, and Great Gable where a four-poster bed and two substantial armchairs overlook the mountains through large windows. A traditional English dinner is served at 7 pm and a house-party atmosphere prevails. John does most of the cooking and a measure of his success is the great number of returning guests, so bookings for one night or bed and breakfast only are not usually accepted. This is walking country so the hotel has a drying room for clothing and is happy to provide packed lunches. *Directions:* The hotel is located 7 miles south of Keswick on the B5289. Turn left over the little humped-back bridge just before entering Rosthwaite village.

HAZEL BANK
Owners: Gwen & John Nuttall
Rosthwaite
Borrowdale
Keswick
Cumbria CA12 5XB, England
Tel: (017687) 77248
6 en-suite rooms
From £43 per person dinner, bed & breakfast
Open mid-March to November
Children over 6
No-smoking house

This solid stone cottage in the tiny village of Rowland is home to Mary Everard and her sleek black labrador Meg. Mary returned to her home area after living in the United States for several years and converted her holiday home into an adorable little bed and breakfast. The large hall, paneled in golden oak with its matching staircase leading to the bedrooms, was once the living room of a much smaller cottage. Warmed in winter by a wood-burning stove, the hall opens up to a country-style dining room with a long polished table and a softly carpeted sitting room with an array of brass fire equipment on the hearth. At the top of the stairs two prettily decorated twin bedrooms with views across the garden share a bath/shower room (with a separate loo). Mary asks guests to select their breakfast the night before so she can have it hot and ready, right on time. Bread is always homemade and yogurt and stewed fruit are available as well as the more usual cooked fare. The nearby Peak District National Park is a walker's paradise and the countryside offers picturesque walled fields and sturdy stone villages, highlighted in the summer when the villagers decorate their wells with floral designs. Also in the vicinity are Bakewell with its antique and tea shops and Monday market, Chatsworth House, and medieval Haddon Hall. *Directions:* Leave Bakewell over the bridge and follow the Hathersage road to Hassop. At Hassop, turn left up the hill for Rowland. After half a mile turn right and Holly Cottage is on the right after two sharp bends.

HOLLY COTTAGE
Owner: Mary Everard
Rowland
Bakewell
Derbyshire DE45 1NR, England
Tel: (01629) 640624
2 rooms, none en suite
From £19 per person
Closed November & December
Children welcome

Rye is a delightful town and we offer Green Hedges as a place to stay if you do not want to be in the quaint, cobbled town center. Set on a very quiet street with private parking (the "no entry" signs discourage non-residents), Green Hedges is a large Edwardian home that has been renovated and refurbished so that guests have one half of the house and Sheila and John Luck and their family have the other. Guests have a small sitting room with games and books (there are televisions in the rooms) and a breakfast room overlooking the large garden which terraces down to a swimming pool and vast expanse of lawn. Breakfast (the only meal served) offers lots of choices including omelets, pancakes with maple syrup, and spicy cheese on wholemeal toast. Upstairs, the three bedrooms are simply decorated and each has a small en-suite shower room. If you prefer a bath, there's a bathroom across the hall. It is a 15-minute walk into town and if you choose to drive, Sheila will direct you along a back-road (go early, parking is scarce). *Directions:* Arrive in Rye on the A268 (London road). Go down Rye Hill and turn right where the circular white sign with red letters states "private road, no entry, no through road." Green Hedges is on your left. (If you cross the railway line, you have gone too far.)

GREEN HEDGES
Owners: Sheila & John Luck
Hillyfields
Rye Hill
Rye
East Sussex TN31 7NH, England
Tel: (01797) 222185
3 en-suite rooms
From £25.50 per person
Closed Christmas
Credit cards: MC, VS
Children over 12
No-smoking house

Rye, a busy port in medieval times, has become marooned 2 miles inland since the sea receded. Once the haunt of smugglers who climbed the narrow cobbled streets laden with booty from France, Rye is now a picturesque town which invites tourists to walk its cobbled lanes. On Rye's most historic street, Jeake's House dates back to 1690 when it was built by Samuel Jeake as a wool storehouse (wool was smuggled to France while brandy, lace, and salt were brought into England). From the street you enter a small reception which leads to a Victorian parlor and bar which opens up to a large galleried hall, now the dining room, where a roaring log fire blazes in winter. At some point in its history the house was owned by the Baptist Church who built this room as a chapel. From the spacious attic bedroom to the romantic four-poster room and the snug single, no two rooms are alike. All are most attractively decorated and furnished with antiques in keeping with the historical mood of the house. All offer modern amenities such as tea-making trays, television, and telephone and all but two have en-suite bathrooms. Within easy driving distance are Winchelsea, Battle Abbey (built on the site of the Battle of Hastings in 1066), Bodiam Castle, and Sissinghurst Gardens. *Directions:* Rye is between Folkestone and Hastings on the A259. Mermaid Street is the main street in town and Jeake's House is near the Mermaid Inn.

JEAKE'S HOUSE
Owners: Jenny & Francis Hadfield
Mermaid Street
Rye
Sussex TN31 7ET, England
Tel: (01797) 222828 Fax: (01797) 222623
12 rooms, 10 en suite
From £20.50 per person
Open all year
Credit cards: all major
Children welcome

Rye is one of England's most enchanting towns and Little Orchard House is one of Rye's most engaging small bed and breakfasts. The location is ideal, right in the heart of town on a small lane leading off Mermaid Street. Don't miss the inn's discreet sign. An archway frames a most inviting little courtyard faced by a pretty cottage with a red-colored door. Inside there is no formal reception area: registration takes place in the cozy, country-style kitchen which opens onto a very large old-fashioned walled garden. In one corner rises a red brick tower, once used by smugglers to signal if the coast was clear. Here there is a spacious ground-floor room and atop the tower a snug, four-poster room with panoramic views. The tower can be rented on a self-catering basis. Bedrooms in the house are equally attractive: Lloyd George is masculine and gracious, the four-poster Garden Room romantic, and the Hayloft cottagey with pine and wicker. The very friendly owners, Sara and Robert, are very involved in the management of their bed and breakfast and personally see that each guest is made welcome and pampered. To learn more about Rye's fascinating history attend the sound and light show at the Rye Town Model, then set out to explore with a walking tour of the town. *Directions:* Follow signs to the town center and enter via the old Landgate Arch. West Street is the third street on the left off the High Street (ignore the "authorized traffic only" signs).

LITTLE ORCHARD HOUSE
Owners: Sara Brinkhurst & Robert Bird
West Street
Rye
Sussex TN31 7ES, England
Tel: (01797) 223831
4 en-suite rooms
From £30 per person
Open all year
Credit cards: MC, VS
Children over 12

Atop the quaint cobbled streets of Rye is the ancient church and churchyard of St. Mary's, surrounded by a square of delightful old houses. Fortunately for visitors to this picturesque town, one of these, The Old Vicarage (a dusty-pink Georgian house with white trim and twin chimneys), is run as a guesthouse by a delightful young couple, Julia and Paul Masters. You can be certain of a proper cuppa here as Julia is a tea-blender and has devised a special blend of tea for her guests. Since Julia and Paul bought The Old Vicarage they have been constantly upgrading and refurbishing the rooms. All of the guestrooms are decorated with Laura Ashley fabrics: two have contemporary four-poster beds and one has a coronet-style draped headboard. Each of the rooms has color television, hairdryer, and tea tray. There are also some small rooms tucked under the eaves on the top floor. The garden suite, a large family room with a sitting area, is below stairs. The ambiance throughout this bed and breakfast is one of homey comfort. Overnight parking is available in a small private car park nearby. If you write ahead, the Masters will send you a brochure with a map on just how to find them amongst the maze of Rye's streets. Rye deserves a visit of several days to explore its narrow, cobbled streets, antique and craft shops, and old fortifications. *Directions:* Rye is on the A259 between Folkestone and Hastings.

THE OLD VICARAGE GUEST HOUSE
Owners: Julia & Paul Masters
66 Church Square
Rye
Sussex TN31 7HF, England
Tel: (01797) 222119 Fax: (01797) 227466
6 rooms, 5 en suite
From £19.50 per person
Closed Christmas
Children over 10

Stratford Lodge is tucked down a quiet lane overlooking a large park just a few minutes' drive from the center of Salisbury. Here Jill Bayly has extended her large Victorian home to create a spacious guesthouse, but her role as caring hostess and the homey touches make Stratford Lodge feel more a large home than a traditional guesthouse. Pretty wallpapers and fabrics, pastel color schemes, antiques, flowers, and family mementos combine to give the bedrooms a home-like charm and all have a tea tray and biscuits, television, and en-suite bathroom. The downstairs twin and the two large upstairs bedrooms that face the park are particular favorites. Three smaller, more modern, double rooms occupy a wing to the rear of the house. Guests are welcome to walk across the garden to swim in the indoor pool. Jill is an excellent cook and offers a dinner menu with choices: she always has at least one fish dish and one vegetarian main course. Breakfast is a treat and, instead of bacon and eggs, guests may try mushrooms on toast or smoked-haddock kedgeree. In addition to Salisbury's old streets and cathedral, Stonehenge and Avebury's megalithic monuments are close at hand while Bath, the New Forest, Winchester, and Southampton are easy day trips. *Directions:* As you enter Salisbury on the A345, from Amesbury, take the second right-hand turn, which is immediately after the Alldays food store, onto Park Lane.

STRATFORD LODGE
Owner: Jill Bayly
4 Park Lane, off Castle Road
Salisbury
Wiltshire SP1 3NP, England
Tel: (01722) 325177 Fax: (01722) 412699
10 en-suite rooms
From £27 per person
Closed Christmas & New Year
Credit cards: all major
Children over 5
No-smoking house

The formal exterior of The Lodge belies the warm decor and friendly welcome which await you indoors. Sally and Roger Dixon's engaging personalities have been imprinted on their home during the three years they spent refurbishing it. Guests can enjoy croquet on the lawn, relax in the Victorian conservatory, or browse through interesting volumes in the comfortable sitting room. Sally is an excellent cook and enjoys serving elaborate dinners in the attractive dining room—the wine list offers a wide selection. The large principal bedroom has a roomy en-suite bathroom while an equally large blue and yellow twin-bedded room shares a spacious bathroom with a snug single bedroom. Sally is very aware that guests always enjoy their own bathroom facilities, so she rents only one of these bedrooms at a time. Nearby Norwich is rich in historic treasures including a beautiful Norman cathedral topped by a 15th-century spire. The castle, built by one of William the Conqueror's supporters is now the Castle Museum. Between Norwich and the holiday resort of Great Yarmouth lie the Norfolk Broads, full of bird life and boating enthusiasts. *Directions:* From Norwich, take the A140 signposted for Ipswich for 6 miles, through the village of Newton Flotman which merges into Saxlingham Thorpe. With Duffields Mill on your right, turn left into Cargate Lane signposted Saxlingham Nethergate, and The Lodge is the second driveway on your left.

THE LODGE
Owners: Sally & Roger Dixon
Cargate Lane
Saxlingham Thorpe
Norwich
Norfolk NR15 1TU, England
Tel: (01508) 471422
3 rooms, 1 en suite
From £24 per person
Closed Christmas
Children over 12

This Suffolk farmhouse stands amidst fields and woods in a quiet country location where for over 400 years it was a working farm. Hostess Mary's caring personality is evident in the quiet, warm way she treats her guests. Her welcome is seconded by handsome, tail-wagging dog Jack and Lizzie, a collie who loves to mother youngsters. Families with children are welcome here, though parents must supervise young ones on the narrow spiral staircase. Mary's old paintings, antique furniture, and books galore fit happily into this mellow, beamed house. Pink-toned armchairs and a long sofa border an Oriental carpet in front of the open log fire in the living room. The food served in the book-lined dining room is excellent: a typical meal might be asparagus and salmon mousse, lamb chops with fresh vegetables and new potatoes, and a choice of desserts. The large principal bedroom has a bathroom en suite while three smaller bedrooms share a bathroom and an additional loo (with a maximum of six guests at a time the facilities are never overtaxed). Nearby are Blythburgh with its 15th-century church, Dunwich, the medieval village almost claimed by the sea, Southwold, Minsmere Bird Reserve, and the concert hall at Snape. *Directions:* From Ipswich take the A12 (signposted Lowestoft). Between Yoxford and Blythburgh take the lane beside The Happy Eater (on the right) and look for High Poplars on the right after 1½ miles.

HIGH POPLARS
Owner: Mary Montague
Hinton
Saxmundham
Suffolk IP17 3RJ, England
Tel: (01502) 478528
3 rooms, 1 en suite
From £22.50 per person
Open all year
Children welcome
Wolsey Lodge

Fronting the picturesque River Teign estuary, Shaldon is a most attractive village where every Wednesday, from May to September, residents dress in 18th-century costume, stalls are set on the green, Morris dancers entertain, and docents give guided tours of the village where the early-17th-century Virginia Cottage is one of the oldest residences. Jennifer and Michael Britton sincerely welcome guests to their home. Visitors have their own sitting room where a log fire burns cheerily in the winter and plump sofas and chairs invite you to curl up with a book or enjoy an evening of television. Breakfast is the only meal served and guests usually walk or drive to the Shipwrights Arms pub or Edens restaurant. The very large double room can accommodate an extra bed and enjoys views over the garden and a large bathroom. One twin-bedded room has an en-suite bathroom while another has its facilities down the hall. If the weather is warm, you can enjoy a refreshing swim in the heated pool. There are lots of National Trust properties within a 30-mile radius. Garden lovers enjoy Plant World where Ray Brown (yes, he's a relative) has planted an interesting geographic garden where each country displays its native plants. *Directions:* From Exeter take the A380 towards Torquay for 3 miles to the B3192 signposted Teignmouth and Shaldon. Cross over the bridge into Shaldon, follow the main road to your right, and turn at once sharp right, signposted Ringmore. Brook Lane is the third lane on the left and Virginia Cottage is on the right.

VIRGINIA COTTAGE
Owners: Jennifer & Michael Britton
Brook Lane
Shaldon
Devon TQ14 0HL, England
Tel & fax: (01626) 872634
3 rooms, 1 en suite
From £21 per person
Open March till December
Babies & children over 10

Longdon Manor is an absolutely delightful home tucked deep in the countryside, fronted by rambling outbuildings and picturesque barns, and backed by a grassy garden whose centerpiece is a tall, 17th-century dovecote. The sitting room invites guests to stretch out in a chair before the log fire, gently play the concert grand, or browse through piles of sheet music and books. The polished flagstones, high ceilings, and deeply set mullioned windows echo days long past, for this was a residence as early as the 14th century, with additions being made in the 16th and 17th centuries. The dining-room walls are hung with family photos, a deep window niche displays fossils and seashells, and the elegant table is laid with country-style crockery. With advance notice Jane is happy to provide dinner. The bedrooms are all different: a cottage-style twin nestles under the eaves and a double room has Jacobean furniture and a flamboyant bathroom. Although Jane does not usually take reservations on weekends, she often accepts guests who would like to attend one of the informal concerts held here once a month. Longdon Manor is perfect for exploring the Cotswold villages and visiting the theater at Stratford-upon-Avon. *Directions:* From Shipston on Stour take the B4035 towards Chipping Campden. Cross the A429 and after half a mile turn right towards Darlingscott. After a mile the lane bends sharp right while the drive to the manor is straight ahead.

LONGDON MANOR
Owners: Jane Brabyn & family
Shipston on Stour
Warwickshire CV36 4PW, England
Tel: (01608) 682235
2 rooms, 1 en suite
From £35 per person
Open April to November, Monday to Thursday
Children welcome
No-smoking house

A cozy hilltop refuge from winter storms, an outstanding spring, summer, or autumn base for exploring Derbyshire by car or on foot, Dannah Farm is a delightful place for all seasons. The solid Georgian farmhouse is turned over entirely to guests with two cozy sitting rooms furnished tastefully and delightful cottagey bedrooms. I particularly liked the two suites which have their private entries from the old stableyard. One has a snug sitting room with an open-tread spiral staircase leading to the low beamed bedroom while the other is a lofty raftered room with a four-poster bed. Another part of the old stables is a convivial bar and country-style restaurant where guests enjoy breakfast and dinner and outside guests are welcomed on Saturday evenings. Adults and children love the animals—the squeaking baby pot-bellied pigs are a great attraction. The Peak District National Park is on your doorstep full of walks, bike trails, and appealing little villages. The stately homes of Haddon Hall and Chatsworth House are well worth a visit. *Directions:* From Belper take the A517 (Ashbourne road) for 2 miles and after the Hanging Gate Inn take the next right (at the top of the hill) to Shottle (1½ miles). Go straight at the crossroads and after 200 yards turn right into Dannah Farm.

DANNAH FARM
Owners: Joan & Martin Slack
Bowmans Lane
Shottle
Belper
Derbyshire DE56 2DR, England
Tel: (01773) 550273 Fax: (01773) 550590
9 rooms, 8 en suite
From £27 per person
Closed Christmas
Credit cards: MC, VS
Children welcome

The Lynch Country House was built for an attorney and his bride in 1812 and was owned by their family for over a hundred years. Roy Copeland purchased the house with the intention of running a country house hotel: however, when the renovations were complete he decided that a bed and breakfast was more his cup of tea. Consequently guests get country-house-style accommodation at bed-and-breakfast prices and Roy gets time to practice his saxophone and clarinet. Roy encourages guests to enjoy the lovely gardens with their topiary hedges and lake with its resident family of black swans. Bedrooms vary in size from snug rooms under the eaves (Alderley is an especially attractive attic room) to Goldington, a large high-ceilinged room with a grand Georgian four-poster bed. Roy supplies a list of restaurants and pubs in each room along with sample menus but finds that guests usually stroll into the village to The Globe pub or Market House restaurant. Somerton, long ago the capital of Wessex, is now a substantial village with some interesting shops and pretty streets lined with old stone houses. Glastonbury, the cradle of English Christianity, and Wells with its magnificent cathedral are nearby. Bath is just under an hour away. *Directions:* Exit the M25 at junction 25, taking the A358 towards Chard to the A378 to Langport and straight on to Somerton.

THE LYNCH COUNTRY HOUSE
Owner: Roy Copeland
4 Behind Berry
Somerton
Somerset TA11 7PD, England
Tel: (01458) 272316 Fax: (01458) 272590
5 rooms, 4 en suite
From £22.50 per person
Open all year
Credit cards: all major
Children welcome

This lovely Georgian home set in 5 acres of grounds in peaceful countryside offers outstanding accommodations. Rashleigh is an enormous room and its double bed has an artfully draped bedhead matching the curtains and bedspread, Treffry is in pink and pine with a frilled corona over the bed, and Prideaux has a dainty, white four-poster bed draped with a pink-and-white flowery fabric. Each bedroom has an elegant en-suite bathroom with spa bath, tea and coffee makings, television, telephone, and a huge umbrella for guests to use during their stay. Guests have their own entrance into a lofty hallway where double doors open up to a vast sitting room all decked out in warm shades of pale green. Beyond lies a sunny conservatory with wicker chairs and little tables set for breakfast or dinner. Outside are vast lawns, a swimming pool, a hot tub, and a paved terrace with spectacular views across rolling countryside. Local attractions include the picturesque town of Fowey, the fishing village of Mevagissey, the cathedral city of Truro, and Bodmin Moor. Daphne Du Maurier's novel *All the King's Men* is set around St. Blazey. *Directions:* Pass over the Tamar Bridge into Cornwall and follow signs to Liskeard. Take the A390 (St. Austell turnoff), following it through Lostwithiel and into St. Blazey. Cross the railway lines and opposite the Texaco garage turn right into Prideaux Road, following it up the hill to Nanscawen on your right.

NANSCAWEN HOUSE
Owners: Janet & Keith Martin
Prideaux Road
St. Blazey, Par
Cornwall PL24 2SR, England
Tel & fax: (01726) 814488
3 en-suite rooms
From £34 per person
Closed Christmas
Credit cards: MC, VS
Children over 12
No-smoking house

Breathtaking, panoramic views of the Wye Valley open up from Cinderhill House, a pink-washed cottage whose core dates back to the 14th century with additions over the years. Gillie is a warm and friendly hostess who enjoys welcoming guests to her lovely home. Bedrooms in the main house are very prettily decorated and all have tea and coffee trays. An additional attic room with twin beds and a crib is reserved for children so that parents can put their children to bed and go downstairs for dinner. Since my visit Gillie has been busy with the conversion of outbuildings to self-catering accommodation or to be used as extra guestrooms for the house. Two of these rooms have four-poster beds and one self-catering unit has been specially equipped to accommodate wheelchairs. Breakfast is a treat: fruit compotes and cold cereals are followed by hot dishes such as fresh salmon fishcakes and herb omelets, yet Gillie considers dinner her forte! On chilly evenings a crackling log fire invites guests into the large sitting room to enjoy a drink before dinner. Apart from enjoying the peace and quiet of the Wye Valley and the Forest of Dean, guests venture farther afield to Bristol, Cardiff, Gloucester, Cheltenham, Bath, and Hereford. *Directions:* Take the M4 from Bristol over the Severn bridge to exit 22 for Monmouth. Follow the A466 for 10 miles, turn right over the Bigsweir bridge for St. Briavels. Follow the road up and the house is on the left just before the castle.

CINDERHILL HOUSE
Owner: Gillie Peacock
St. Briavels
Gloucestershire GL15 6HR, England
Tel: (01594) 530393 Fax: (01594) 530098
5 en-suite rooms
From £24 per person
Open all year
Children welcome

Hilltop has been in host Tim Rathmell's family since it was built in 1640: quite an impressive record! Tim and his wife, Marie Louise, have tastefully modernized the house adding en-suite bathrooms while keeping and exposing lovely features such as the beef loft in the beamed dining room where beef used to be hung to dry above the open fire. They have made the old barn into their home and enjoy welcoming guests to the main house. Four bedrooms with light and airy decor contain spacious king-sized beds and have showers in the bathrooms. The fifth bedroom is a snug, flowery twin and enjoys a large bathroom with a claw-foot tub. Ancient family documents decorate the tiny bar where guests gather to chat over drinks. Dinner is served on Fridays and Saturdays when Tim puts his heart into his cooking and concentrates on properly cooked vegetables and sauces to accompany his main courses while Marie Louise is in charge of dessert which may be a specialty from her German homeland. After dinner guests enjoy the cheer of a blazing log fire in the sitting room or, on warm summer evenings, stretch their legs strolling in the foothills behind Hilltop or down to the village pub. Walks abound in this lovely part of the Yorkshire Dales, and car touring is just as enjoyable, offering castles, country homes, and abbeys. A scenic 70-mile round-trip route from Hilltop includes Kilnsey Crag, Malham Tarn, Gordale Scar, and Stump Cross caverns. *Directions:* Starbotton is in Wharfedale, 16 miles north of Skipton on the B6160.

HILLTOP COUNTRY GUEST HOUSE
Owners: Marie Louise & Tim Rathmell
Starbotton
Skipton
North Yorkshire BD23 5HY, England
Tel: (01756) 760321
5 en-suite rooms
From £25 per person
Open mid-March to mid-November
Children welcome

Only the most detailed maps pinpoint Curdon Mill in the hamlet of Vellow, but your endeavors to find this lovely valley close to the sea and near the beautiful Quantock hills are rewarded. The approach to the mill skirts Daphne and Richard Criddle's farm. A few years ago they decided to renovate the old water mill on their property, adding a lounge where guests can relax and browse through books describing sights to see in the area. The mill shaft hangs across the ceiling in the dining room and the restaurant is open to the public (restaurant closed Sundays). The menu changes daily and there are at least four choices of starter, main, and dessert courses. The cheeses are all English and local. Of the six bedrooms my favorites are the Stag Room which was named because deer can sometimes be seen in the fields below the window and the Walnut Room, named for the walnut bedheads. A small swimming pool is secluded on a terrace beside the mill. It's a rural spot where you can enjoy watching the farm animals, taking walks, or even trout fishing. Exmoor National Park is nearby, a region of spectacular scenery which varies from farmland to heathland. *Directions:* Leave the M25 at Taunton, junction 25, and take the A358 towards Williton. Do not turn left until you see Stogumber and Vellow signpost together. Curdon Mill is on a sharp right-hand bend before you reach Stogumber.

CURDON MILL
Owners: Daphne & Richard Criddle
Lower Vellow, Stogumber
Taunton
Somerset TA4 4LS, England
Tel: (01984) 656522 Fax: (01984) 656197
6 en-suite rooms
From £25 per person
Open all year
Credit cards: all major
Children over 10
No-smoking house

The food at The Angel Inn is outstanding and, fortunately for visitors to this pretty part of Suffolk, guests may lodge as well as dine here. When Peter Smith and Richard Wright purchased the inn in 1985 it was in a sorry state, but now its complete refurbishment has transformed it into a building with lots of charm and old-world ambiance. Guests eating in the bar on the weekends (best advised to avoid the crush by arriving early or just before last orders at 9 pm) make their selection from the menu hung on the old red-brick wall above the fireplace and then settle down at one of the tables grouped under the low beamed ceiling. Those who prefer a quieter atmosphere may elect to dine in the restaurant where tables can be reserved in either of the two dining rooms. One is a cozy room with pine paneling, the other more dramatic, with ceilings removed to expose lofty rafters. Tables are laid with linen and soft lighting adds a romantic mood. The menu offers several choices of starters and main courses including a good selection of fresh seafood. Bedrooms are pleasantly furnished and have a light, airy decor. This unspoilt region of quiet countryside offers lots of sightseeing, such as the nearby valley of the River Stour, Dedham, and Flatford Mill, all made famous by John Constable's paintings. *Directions:* Take the A134 Sudbury road from Colchester for 5 miles to Nayland, then turn left for the 2-mile-drive to Stoke by Nayland.

THE ANGEL INN
Owners: Richard Wright & Peter Smith
Stoke by Nayland, Colchester
Essex CO6 4SA, England
Tel: (01206) 263245 Fax: (01206) 337324
6 en-suite rooms
From £28.75 per person
Closed Christmas
Credit cards: all major
Children over 12

There is a moat most of the way round Slough Court, a 14th-century fortified manor house with tiny mullioned windows set in mellow stone walls beneath a moss-covered roof. Enclosed by the moat is a garden of rolling lawns and overflowing flowerbeds, a grass tennis court, and a sheltered swimming pool. Across the drawbridge lies the farmyard full of barns and tractors, pigs and cows. Sally is the fourth generation of her family to call Slough Court home, a home which she thoroughly enjoys sharing with her guests. Opposite the great hall with its enormous fireplace is the elegant dining room, the table prettily laid for breakfast with the cereals displayed in giant glass jars. In summer breakfast is the only meal served and guests either walk to the village pub or drive to The Rising Sun, in Knapp, which specializes in fresh fish cuisine. Up the narrow staircase, heavy old doors open to attractive bedrooms with tiny paned windows and exposed wall beams (two are en suite and one has its bathroom down the hall). If you are interested in farm activities, you can watch the cows being milked and discuss the finer points of raising pigs. Basket-making is a traditional Somerset craft and several local farms offer demonstrations and sell baskets. Farther afield lie the towns of Glastonbury and Wells. *Directions:* From Taunton take the A358 towards Chard to the A378 where you turn left towards Langport. In 200 yards turn left onto a country lane signposted North Curry and Stoke St. Gregory. Slough Court is on the left in Slough Lane.

SLOUGH COURT
Owner: Sally Gothard
Stoke St. Gregory
Taunton
Somerset TA3 6JQ, England
Tel & fax: (01823) 490311
3 rooms, 2 en suite
From £23.50 person
Open March to November
Children over 12

Bretton House sits beside Fosse Way, the ancient Roman road that runs straight as an arrow through the heart of the Cotswolds. Isolated from the busy thoroughfare by 2 acres of garden, Bretton House was built at the turn of the century as a rectory. The vicar certainly enjoyed an inspirational view of gently rolling Cotswold countryside from his large rambling home. Julia and Barry bought the house specifically to provide bed and breakfast—putting to good use Barry's training as a cook and his experience managing pubs and restaurants. A pretty pine dining room has little tables and chairs set before tall windows which open up to the garden and the countryside views. For relaxation there is both a smoking and non-smoking sitting room. Up the broad staircase, the bedrooms are named for their decor: Peach has a frilly four-poster, Sweet Pea has airy flowers on the fabric and wallpaper and lovely countryside views, and Fuchsia has blue-fuchsia-covered draperies and bedspreads. All have en-suite facilities. Ask to see the enormous fluffy St. Bernards, Megan and Jessie, whose "home" is one of the outbuildings. Bretton House provides an ideal base for exploring the Cotswolds—within an hour you can be in Stratford-upon-Avon, Warwick, or Oxford. *Directions:* From Stow-on-the-Wold, take the A429 towards Cirencester. Pass a garage on your right and a cemetery on your left, and Bretton House is on your left at the brow of the hill.

BRETTON HOUSE
Owners: Julia & Barry Allen
Fosseway
Stow-on-the-Wold
Gloucestershire GL54 1JU, England
Tel: (01451) 830388
3 en-suite rooms
From £20 per person
Closed Christmas
Children over 10

Alveston Cottage began life over 400 years ago as two one-up-one-down cottages by the River Avon in the heart of Stratford-upon-Avon. Victorian additions melded the tiny dwellings into one and more recently Louise Downing has added her skills to make this unusual house into the most inviting of homes, a home she loves to share with guests. Louise is particularly proud of her art collection where each piece is done by a person she interviewed in the course of her career as a journalist with *The Times*. Louise particularly enjoys preparing old English recipes and offers either dinner or pre-theater supper, serving them in the little parlor with its views through willow branches of the Avon. Upstairs, the bedrooms enjoy an uninterrupted view of the river and are particularly attractive with their white-on-white decor and lacy Victorian pillows. One has an en-suite bathroom while the other has robes provided for trotting to its private bathroom down the hall. Theater tickets can be arranged and Alveston Cottage is just a few minutes' walk from the Royal Shakespeare Theatre. All the attractions of Stratford (except Anne Hathaway's cottage) are within easy walking distance. Advance reservations are essential. *Directions:* From Oxford take the A34 to Stratford. Before crossing the bridge into town, turn right (B4086 to Wellesbourne) opposite the Forte Posthouse (Swan's Nest Hotel) and Alveston Cottage is the first house on the riverside.

ALVESTON COTTAGE
Owner: Louise Downing
Tiddington Road
Stratford-upon-Avon
Warwickshire CV37 7AE, England
Tel: (01789) 292847
2 rooms, 1 en suite
From £32 per person
Open April to October
Children over 12

Set behind Tansley village green, Lane End House is, as its name states, the last house in the lane. A house which has been considerably expanded, with a large sitting room whose picture window overlooks the garden. Marion and David Smith used to run a large hotel in Leicestershire and they apply the same professional standards to their guesthouse. Food here is low in fat and sugar. Dinner offers choices in all but the main course, and catering to vegetarians is not a problem. David's wine list is extensive. At breakfast time, there's homemade muesli, fruit compote, a fresh fruit platter, and bacon and sausages from the local butcher. A ground-floor bedroom has its bathroom just a few steps away across the hallway. An open-tread staircase leads up from the dining room to a further three bedrooms, where quite the nicest one has as coronet bedhead draped with pink-and-green fabric and a bathroom with a claw-foot tub and old-fashioned toilet with its cistern almost at ceiling level. *Directions:* From Matlock, take the A615 Alfreton road for 1½ miles. Enter Tansley village and turn left before the Tavern pub into Church Street. After 500 yards when you see the Gate Inn in front of you, turn right into Green Lane and Lane End House is at the end of the lane

LANE END HOUSE
Owners: Marion & David Smith
Green Lane
Tansley
Matlock
Derbyshire DE4 5FJ, England
Tel: (01629) 583981
4 rooms, 2 en suite
From £21 per person
Open all year
Credit cards: MC, VS
Children welcome
No-smoking house

Thomas Luny, the marine artist, had this home built in 1792 in the center of Teignmouth just a short walk through narrow streets from the sheltered harbor which has a long history as a fishing and ship-building center. Now this handsome house is home to Alison and John Allan and their two young children. John serves guests pre-dinner drinks before donning the starched white uniform that both he and Alison wear for serving dinner. In the morning John or Alison brings early morning tea to your room. All the rooms have an en-suite bathroom, a television, mineral water, and a lovely old sea chest. Each is decorated in a contrasting style: Chinese enjoys a peach-and-green decor and painted Oriental furniture; Clairmont is pretty in green and yellow; Luny is autumnal in beige and brown; and Bitton contemporary with its impressive four-poster bed. Walk the narrow streets of old Teignmouth to the working harbor and along to the Victorian section of town with its long sandy beach, cheerful pier, and esplanade popular with the bucket-and-spade brigade. Just across the estuary lies Shaldon where every Wednesday, from May to September, residents dress in 18th-century costume. *Directions:* From Exeter take the A380 towards Torquay for 3 miles to the B3192 to Teignmouth. Turn left at the traffic lights at the bottom of the hill, then turn immediately right signposted Quays, and immediately left into Teign Street. Thomas Luny House is on your right.

THOMAS LUNY HOUSE
Owners: Alison & John Allan
Teign Street
Teignmouth
Devon TQ14 8EG, England
Tel: (01626) 772976
4 en-suite rooms
From £30 per person
Closed January
Children over 12
Wolsey Lodge

When I saw Brattle House, clad with weatherboard and mellow Kent peg tile, it looked like an ordinary home, so I was thrilled to enter the wide pine front door and discover that the house dates back to the 1600s and is delightful in every way. The cozy, oak-beamed sitting room opens up to a conservatory where afternoon tea and breakfast are served. Glasses and ice are provided so that guests can bring their own alcohol to enjoy drinks before, during, and after dinner which is eaten by candlelight round an antique mahogany table. Mo and Alan Rawlinson join guests, after the first course, for convivial evenings of dining and conversation. Up the wide staircase, two spacious front bedrooms enjoy broad window seats overlooking the fields to the distant church tower, but I must admit that my heart was won by the cozy little back bedroom with its idyllic view across the garden to open countryside. The Rawlinsons' most popular (fine-weather) excursion (apart from nearby Sissinghurst Castle and gardens) involves taking the old Kent and West Sussex steam train from Tenterden (past the house) to Northiam, then a little wooden ferry to Bodiam Castle, where you enjoy tea at Knollys before touring the castle. *Directions:* From Tenterden, take the A28 towards Hastings for a short distance, go down the hill and turn right towards Cranbrook. Brattle House is on the left after ¼ mile.

BRATTLE HOUSE
Owners: Mo & Alan Rawlinson
Watermill Bridges
Tenterden
Kent TN30 6UL, England
Tel: (01580) 763565
3 en-suite rooms
From £26.50 per person
Closed Christmas & New Year
Children over 15
No-smoking house
Wolsey Lodge

Theberton Grange has grown over the years so that you find cozy little rooms that date back to Tudor times alongside spacious, high-ceilinged Victorian rooms. Dawn and Paul purchased the house, which had been converted to a hotel, in a state of disrepair and have worked hard to restore it—the garden with its wild wooded dell and masses of spring daffodils is neat and tidy, the patio has been relaid, and the interior has been decorated. Signs of former times remain in the numbers on the bedroom doors and the fire doors which were installed without a thought to the age of the building. The most attractive guestroom is the master bedroom (1), a spacious Victorian room with views on two sides to the garden. Two of the bedrooms have their bathrooms directly across the hall. Paul has always cooked for a hobby and is quickly expanding his considerable skills. Paul and Dawn are easy-going and welcoming and ready to offer advice on where to go and what to see. On the coast Aldeburgh has delightful Georgian houses and its local council still meets in the half-timbered Moot Hall (1512). At Snape Maltings a collection of red-brick granaries and old malthouses has been converted into a riverside center with interesting shops and a concert hall, home of the Aldeburgh music festival. *Directions:* From Ipswich take the A12 (Lowestoft) to Yoxford and turn right on the B1122 to Leiston. Pass through Theberton village and immediately after leaving the village turn right (signposted Kelsale): Theberton Grange is on your left.

THEBERTON GRANGE   **NEW**
Owners: Dawn & Paul Rosher
Theberton near Leiston
Suffolk IP16 4RR, England
Tel & fax: (01728) 830625
7 rooms, 5 en suite
From £32.50 per person
Closed Christmas
Credit cards: all major
Children over 7

After working for many years in the south of England, Pat and Ted Hesketh decided they needed a change of pace, their objective being to live in a quiet village where they could see hills. They made a perfect choice in High Green House, sitting beside the village green in the little village of Thoralby nestled in the peace and quiet of Bishopdale which connects the busier Yorkshire dales of Wharfedale and Wensleydale. Guests enjoy a comfortable sitting room with a cheery log fire on cool evenings. Pat is happy to provide a well priced three-course dinner with a choice of starters and desserts should guests want to eat in. The largest bedroom (a double) has a spectacular view of the hillsides dotted with tiny stone barns and its private bathroom is just next door. The smaller twin-bedded room has a snug en-suite bathroom. A ground-floor bedroom with a large en-suite shower room is equipped for disabled guests. Pat and Ted are happy to assist in planning walking and driving tours through the stunning scenery made famous by the Herriot television series. To experience some magnificent scenery, take a breathtaking circular drive from Thoralby up Bishopdale, over Kidstones Pass into Wharfedale, thence by Littondale and over the fells to Malham Cove. Return either via Ribblesdale and Hawes or via Grassington. *Directions:* Turn south to Thoralby from the A684 just east of Aysgarth village. Upon entering Thoralby, High Green House is on your right next to the village shop.

HIGH GREEN HOUSE   **NEW**
Owners: Pat & Ted Hesketh
Thoralby, Leyburn
North Yorkshire DL8 3SU, England
Tel & fax: (01969) 663420
3 rooms, 2 en suite
From £26 per person
Open mid-March to October
Credit cards: MC, VS
Children over 10

Littleburn is a fine early-Georgian small country house dating from about 1700 in a lovely setting in the Yorkshire Dales National Park. Diana and Donald Cameron have lived all over the world and have always enjoyed entertaining and welcoming visitors: the only difference nowadays is that guests are paying bed-and-breakfast patrons. Early arrivals are welcomed with tea, shown to their rooms, and invited to join Donald and Diana for pre-dinner drinks in the drawing room which, paneled in old pine and overlooking green fields and hills across the lawn, is a particularly attractive room. In the dining room the elegant table is laid with Waterford crystal and silver service. After dinner, guests are settled in the drawing room to be joined for conversation and drinks by their hosts and the friendly King Charles spaniels, Sophie and Poppy, who affectionately vie for visitors' attentions. On chilly evenings an open log fire adds cheer to the occasion. There are many spots to visit including Aysgarth Falls, Malham Tarn, Hardraw Falls, Jervaulx Abbey, Fountains Abbey, and Newby Hall and gardens. *Directions:* Turn south to Thoralby from the A684 just east of Aysgarth village. Upon entering Thoralby, turn right at the post office/shop onto a minor road. Pass the George Inn on the right and bear left at the next fork for Littleburn: the house is on the right just after the little bridge.

LITTLEBURN
Owners: Diana & Donald Cameron
Thoralby
Leyburn
North Yorkshire DL8 3BE, England
Tel: (01969) 663621
3 en-suite rooms
From £29 per person
Closed Christmas
Children not accepted
Wolsey Lodge

Thornton Watlass is a delightful Wharfedale village set amongst gently rolling farmland where quiet, narrow lanes lead you to the heart of the magnificent Yorkshire Dales. How fortunate that this lovely spot offers an award-winning bed and breakfast, The Old Rectory, a substantial Georgian home decked with wisteria, roses, and jasmine just at the edge of the village green. Olivia and Richard Farnell are justifiably proud that they won the prestigious English Tourist Board "England for Excellence" award in 1992. Olivia is the talented seamstress and decorator responsible for the enviable decor of softly hued sponged walls complementing the beautiful fabrics. The premier bedroom has a spectacular, softly draped half-tester bed and en-suite bathroom. The blue double room and spacious twin, decorated in pale shades of yellow and green, share a large bathroom and a smaller shower room ensuring that guests always have private facilities. Guests have their own immaculate sitting room where a log fire burns in the winter and they can enjoy complimentary tea and crumpets. Breakfast is the only meal served and Olivia and Richard spoil you for choice with their suggestions of restaurants and pubs. Arm yourself with one of the Farnells' driving routes that guide you through the Yorkshire Dales. *Directions:* From Bedale take the B6268 towards Masham and Thornton Watlass is signposted to your right down 2½ miles of narrow country lanes.

THE OLD RECTORY
Owners: Olivia & Richard Farnell
Thornton Watlass
Nr Masham
Yorkshire HG4 4AH, England
Tel & fax: (01677) 423456
3 rooms, 1 en suite
2-night minimum
From £32.50 per person
Open all year
Children over 12

The huge stone cheese presses in the McGinns' paddock mark the border between England and Wales, making this an ideal base for your explorations of North Wales and for visits to the walled Roman town of Chester. Valerie and John McGinn have done the most incredible job of converting what was previously a Georgian stable block into a lovely home. Guest accommodation is offered in three delightful ground-floor rooms each accompanied by a sparkling en-suite bathroom. Two bedrooms open up to private patios, while a third offers wheelchair access from the cobbled courtyard. In warmer weather, guests breakfast in the spacious conservatory whose windows open to views of the large fish pond and pretty countryside views across the ha-ha. Guests are welcome to use the sheltered tennis court or enjoy croquet on the lawn. South Cheshire is renowned for cheese making and you can visit local producers and watch cheese being made by traditional methods. *Directions:* From Chester, take the A41 towards Whitchurch. At the New Inn pub, turn right onto B5069 to Malpas. Turn left and then the first right at The Crown pub towards Wrexham. After 3 miles, pass a small filling station and the red-brick wall which borders Broughton House which is on your left before you reach the signpost for Clywd.

BROUGHTON HOUSE
Owners: Valerie & John McGinn
Threapwood
Malpas
Cheshire SY14 7AN, England
Tel & fax: (01948) 770610
3 en-suite rooms
From £27 per person
Closed Christmas
Children over 10
No-smoking house

From a country road just off the A1 (London to Scotland road), you sweep down a gravel driveway to Tickencote Hall, a grand, mellow-stone manor surrounded by acres of parkland backing onto the tiny village of Tickencote with its quaint stone cottages. Dating from 1705, Tickencote Hall is home to Tarn and Peter Dearden and their three grown sons. I found the drawing room and dining room to be the height of country-house elegance and the sunny bedrooms are prettily decorated in bright chintz fabrics and furnished with antique furniture—although the comfortable beds are new. The Hall is run on traditional Wolsey Lodge house-party lines, with guests gathering for drinks in the drawing room before dining together. Nearby Stamford, with its fine Georgian buildings and narrow alleyways full of interesting antique shops, pubs, and restaurants is a "must visit." In summer there's open-air Shakespearean theater at nearby Tolethorpe. Tarn is happy to supply a picnic for this, or provide two courses of dinner before the performance and two courses on your return. *Directions:* Take the A1 north to the Stamford roundabout, continue north on the A1 for 4 miles passing two left turns and the Tickencote sign, and turn left into the Texaco garage. Cross the forecourt and turn right towards Tickencote, ignoring the "Village Only" sign. Tickencote Hall's drive is on your left after 15 yards, opposite a bus shelter.

TICKENCOTE HALL
Owners: Tarn & Peter Dearden
Tickencote
Stamford
Lincolnshire PE9 4AE, England
Tel & fax: (01780) 65155
4 rooms, 2 en suite
From £35 per person
Closed Christmas
Credit cards: MC, VS
Children over 12
Wolsey Lodge

Claiming the honor of being King Arthur's legendary birthplace, the ruins of Tintagel Castle cling to a wild headland exposed to the coastal winds. It's a place of myths that attracts visitors who come to soak up its fanciful past and enjoy its rugged scenery. While the village of Tintagel is a touristy spot, just a mile away lies the quiet hamlet of Trenale, a cluster of cottages, and the delightful Trebrea Lodge. Behind the impressive, tall Georgian façade lies a much older building of cozy, comfortable rooms. Upstairs the drawing room is full of splendid antiques but you will probably find yourself downstairs toasting your toes by the fire enveloped by a large armchair, enjoying drinks and coffee after a delicious dinner in the paneled dining room with its views across stone-walled fields to the distant sea. We particularly enjoyed our room (4) furnished, as are all the rooms, with lovely antiques and enjoying a large bathroom, the four-poster room (1) with its ornately carved Victorian four-poster bed, and room 5, a delightful twin-bedded room with its view to the distant ocean. A tempting array of hot breakfast dishes is placed on the buffet for guests to help themselves. Walkers enjoy spectacular cliff-top walks along rugged headlands. To the north lies Clovelly. *Directions:* From Tintagel take the road towards Boscastle and at the edge of the village turn right at the contemporary-style church. Turn right at the top of the lane and Trebrea Lodge is on your left.

TREBREA LODGE
Owners: John Charlick & Sean Devlin
Trenale, Tintagel
Cornwall PL34 0HR, England
Tel: (01840) 770410 Fax: (01840) 770092
7 en-suite rooms
From £34 per person
Closed January 8–31
Children over 9
Smoking in one public room

Marjorie and Euan Aitken's home is a picture-book thatched cottage in an idyllically quiet Oxfordshire village, nestled beside a duck pond with a rowboat moored beneath overhanging willows. When the Aitkens restored the cottage they preserved all the lovely old features they uncovered: an old range and copper boiler, beams with the carpenter's identification marks, and a pump. Every room is furnished with antiques and decorated with collections of bric-a-brac and country bygones. Across the farmyard the timbered barn has been converted to provide six immaculate guestrooms with modern showers, televisions, exposed beams, and displays of Marjorie's collections. I particularly enjoyed Mary (the rooms are named after royals), its corridor hung with farm implements, a Cumberland quilt decorating the bedroom wall, and its choirboy-vestments cupboard used as a closet. Breakfast is the only meal served in the country-pine breakfast room. The milking shed next door is in the process of being converted into two more en-suite ground-floor bedrooms. Oxford colleges, less than half an hour away, are a popular sightseeing spot, as is Blenheim Palace. Nearby Waddesden Manor, the ancestral Rothschild home, has a spectacular art collection. *Directions:* Exit the M40 at junction 6 and take the B4009 to Chinnor where you turn left on the B4445 towards Thame. After 2 miles turn right to Towersey, right at the crossroads, and the farm is on your left at the end of the village.

UPPER GREEN FARM
Owners: Marjorie & Euan Aitken
Manor Road
Towersey
Oxon OX9 3QR, England
Tel: (01844) 212496 Fax: (01844) 260399
10 en-suite rooms
From £20 per person
Open all year
Children over 13
No-smoking house

Pat and Richard Mason transformed a tumbledown cottage and barn in an overgrown field by a stream into a delightful home facing a pretty lake with an idyllic garden full of unusual plants. Inside, the house is just as attractive as out. Sofas are drawn up around the wood-burning stove in the beamed sitting room. Upstairs, the two bedrooms are adjacent to each other and a shower room that has a super-large cubicle. The three rooms handily make into a family suite. When there are two parties of guests, the large double room has the private use of the shower room while the small blue twin has the private use of an additional bathroom down the hall. Breakfast is the only meal served: guests sometimes walk to the local pub for dinner, but more often than not they drive to the Mayfly pub which offers good food and a pretty view of the River Test. One of Pat's suggested day trips is to visit the national rose collection at Mottisfont Abbey, Hilliers Arboretum, and Broadlands, the home of the late Lord Mountbatten. Salisbury and Winchester are 15 miles distant. *Directions:* From the A303, at Andover, take the A3057 (Stockbridge road) and turn first right, signposted for Upper Clatford. Take the first left, go right at the T-junction, and turn right opposite the Crook and Shears pub into a little lane which leads to Malt Cottage.

MALT COTTAGE
Owners: Pat & Richard Mason
Upper Clatford
Andover
Hampshire SP11 7QL, England
Tel: (01264) 323469 Fax: (01264) 334100
2 rooms, none en suite
From £18.50 per person
Closed Christmas
Children welcome

Upton House, a 12th-century manor house, offers guests a winning combination: a lovely house with country-cottage coziness, outstanding decor, treasured antiques, carefully tended, flower-filled gardens, and a charming hostess. In the sitting room plump sofas covered in soft-pink or blue brocade are grouped before the fireplace. In the adjacent dining room soft-primrose walls highlight the ancient beams and a log fire blazes in the fireplace whose ornate pine mantle is decked with delicate china. From the dining room a private staircase leads to the Green Bedroom, a twin-bedded room where everything from the tiny flowered bag containing guest soap to the pretty floral curtains coordinates with the muted pink walls, while up the main cottage staircase are two equally lovely rooms. All have tea caddies packed with every imaginable type of tea, fine china gracing the tea trays, and bathrooms supplied with every extra. Dinner is available with advance reservations. There are enough activities nearby to occupy a week and the Jeffersons have maps marked for exploration of the Elgar Trail, Shakespeare country, and the Cotswolds. The nearby Royal Worcester porcelain factory seconds shop is a favorite with guests. *Directions:* Upton Snodsbury is 6 miles east of Worcester on the A422 to Stratford. Turn right by the Red Lion on the B4082 towards Pershore: Upton House is by the church

UPTON HOUSE
Owners: Angela & Hugh Jefferson
Upton Snodsbury
Worcester
Worcestershire WR7 4NR, England
Tel: (01905) 381226
3 en-suite rooms
From £32.50 per person
Closed Christmas & New Year
Children not accepted
Wolsey Lodge

On every research trip we find a very special place to stay and in 1992 it was **Beryl, a** Gothic revival mansion on 13 acres of grounds. Special not only because of its location, just a mile from Wells cathedral, or because it is a beautifully decorated home full of lovely antiques, but because of the special way that Holly and Eddie give of themselves to their guests. The measure of their success is the number of returning guests who bring their family, friends, and even dogs (provided that they are compatible with the resident chocolate labs). Lovers of elegant antiques will delight in every nook and cranny of Beryl—Eddie is a well-known antique dealer. All the bedrooms have special features. We loved our room, Summer, all pretty in pink and white with daisies on the wallpaper and bedcovers. Next door, Spring has an elegantly draped four-poster bed to leap (literally) into. Choose Winston if you have a passion for grand, old-fashioned, climb-into bathtubs; Butterfly if you enjoy space and want to wake up with Wells cathedral framed in the enormous bay window. Wells is England's smallest city, with the most glorious cathedral. *Directions:* Leave or approach Wells on the B3139 in the direction of Radstock. Turn into Hawkers Lane (not Beryl Lane) opposite the BP garage. Drive to the top of the lane and continue straight into Beryl's driveway.

BERYL
Owners: Holly & Eddie Nowell
Hawkers Lane
Wells
Somerset BA5 3JP, England
Tel: (01749) 678738 Fax: (01749) 670508
6 en-suite rooms
From £32.50 per person
Closed Christmas
Credit cards: MC, VS
Children welcome
Wolsey Lodge

Built in 1280 by monks from the Wilmington Priory, this parsonage is reputedly the oldest small medieval house still inhabited in England. The outside walls are of flint with green stone dressing, while the inside are constructed of blocks of chalk supporting huge oak beams and are studded with little leaded windows and narrow wooden doors. On chilly mornings, guests enjoy breakfast at little tables set before a blazing log fire in the baronial sitting room. A narrow stone staircase winds up from here to the Hall, where a four-poster bed sits beneath a high timbered ceiling. The Solar is also accessed by way of a narrow spiral staircase. Here little windows open to views of the adjacent churchyard and the bed sits beneath a beautiful wooden ceiling. All the bath/shower rooms are in a part of the house that was added in Victorian times, so guests have to pad down the halls to reach their private bathrooms. A popular day hike takes you through the surrounding forest to East Dean, along the famous Seven Sisters chalk cliffs, and back to West Dean. Glynebourne is a 20-minute drive away. *Directions:* From Brighton, take the A27 (Eastbourne road) past Lewes and after a 20-minute drive turn right towards Alfriston, left to Litleton, right at the T-junction towards East Dean, and left following the narrow one-way road through the hamlet to The Old Parsonage beside the church.

THE OLD PARSONAGE
Owners: Angela & Raymond Woodhams
West Dean
Alfriston, nr Seaford
East Sussex BN25 4AL, England
Tel: (01323) 870432
3 rooms, none en suite
From £25 per person
Closed Christmas & New Year
Children over 12
No-smoking house

The Citadel sits like a mighty fortress on a knoll overlooking verdant countryside. As soon as you cross the threshold you realize this is not a "castle" of drafty halls and stone chambers, but a lovely home built to a fanciful design. A spacious sitting room occupies one of the turrets and leads to the large billiard room. Sylvia and her husband, Beverley, often join guests for sherry before dinner and then guests dine together round the long dining-room table. You are welcome to bring your own wine. Up the broad staircase, two of the bedrooms occupy turrets. I particularly enjoyed the one at the front of the house with its adjacent Victorian-style bathroom with center-stage claw-foot tub. A small twin-bedded room has an en-suite shower room. The adjacent golf club is a popular venue, but the real magic of the area lies in a visit to Hawkstone Park where you follow an intricate network of pathways through woodlands and across a narrow log bridge to high cliffs, a ruined castle, mystical grotto, and giant obelisk. The Ironbridge Gorge Museums, Shrewsbury, and Chester are within an hour's drive. *Directions:* From Shrewsbury, take the A49 (north) for 12 miles, turn right for Hodnet and Weston-under-Redcastle, and The Citadel is on your right, a quarter of a mile after leaving Weston-under-Redcastle (before Hawkstone Park).

THE CITADEL
Owners: Sylvia & Beverley Griffiths
Weston-under-Redcastle
Shrewsbury
Shropshire SY4 5JY, England
Tel & fax: (01630) 685204
3 rooms, 1 en suite
From £32.50 per person
Open April to November
Children over 12
No-smoking house
Wolsey Lodge

Willersey's duck pond sits on the village green overlooked by golden-stone cottages. The little lane that runs beside the pub leads to The Old Rectory, sitting in a spacious garden with the 11th-century village church as its closest neighbor. The mulberry tree in the garden is reputed to have been planted in the reign of Queen Elizabeth I and still provides fruit and jam for breakfast. Bedrooms in The Old Rectory come in all shapes and sizes, from a snug attic room where bathrobes are provided for padding across the hall to grander en-suite rooms with four-poster beds. If you want complete privacy, opt for either the Bridle or Saddle rooms found in the converted stables overlooking the lovely garden. Bedrooms have everything from color television to quality toiletries. Individual tables are set for breakfast. In the evening guests usually stroll down to the Bell for dinner (flashlights are provided for guiding your way home). The Old Rectory is a perfect base for touring the pretty Cotswold villages and visiting manor houses and gardens. A delightful day trip takes you farther afield to Stratford-upon-Avon and Warwick Castle. *Directions:* From Broadway take the B4632 towards Stratford-upon-Avon for 1½ miles to Willersey. Turn right into Church Street at the Bell, and The Old Rectory is at the end of the lane.

THE OLD RECTORY
Owners: Liz & Chris Beauvoisin
Church Street
Willersey, Broadway
Worcestershire WR12 7PN, England
Tel: (01386) 853729 Fax: (01386) 858061
8 rooms, 6 en suite
From £30 per person
Closed Christmas
Credit cards: MC, VS
Children over 8
No-smoking house

One of the attractions for garden lovers staying at Tavern House is that Westonbirt Arboretum with its 600 acres of trees is just down the road. Although the house sits right beside the A433 there is no noise problem–thick walls and double glazing do the job in the daytime and the road is quiet at night. Breakfast is the only meal served at the cottagey little tables and chairs in the dining room and for dinner guests often go to the nearby village of Sherton to the Rattlebowne Inn or the Carpenters Arms. A log fire is lit in the guests' sitting room on cool evenings. All of the bedrooms are very private as each of the four rooms has its own narrow little staircase. Room 1 is especially spacious with its high beamed ceiling rising to the rafters, a small dressing room (ideal for parking large cases), and a bathroom large enough to accommodate a bath and separate shower. Janet and Tim used to own a large hotel in Salcombe and they have applied the same professional standards to their bed and breakfast venture. Sightseeing within a 25-mile radius includes the little market town of Chipping Sodbury; Badmington House, a superb Palladian mansion in a 52,000-acre estate; the market town of Cirencester; Cheltenham with its Regency houses; Slimbridge Wild Fowl Trust; and Berkeley Castle. *Directions:* Leave the M4 at junction 18, take the A46 (Stroud, Cirencester) to the A433 towards Tetbury. Tavern House is on your right 1 mile before Westonbirt Arboretum. Park in the lane and ring the front door bell, or use the outdoor phone.

TAVERN HOUSE **NEW**
Owners: Janet & Tim Tremellen
Willesley, near Tetbury
Gloucestershire GLS 8QU, England
Tel: (01666) 880444 Fax: (01666) 880254
4 en-suite rooms
From £29.50 per person
Open all year
Credit cards: MC, VS
Children over 10

Stratford-upon-Avon is a mecca for visitors who come for everything associated with Shakespeare: the performances of his plays, the town's Tudor buildings, Anne Hathaway's cottage, and Mary Arden's house. Just across the garden from Mary Arden's house you find Pear Tree Cottage, home to Margaret and Ted Mander for almost forty years, a home which has been sympathetically extended to provide seven en-suite bedrooms for guests. All the rooms are delightful, though I particularly enjoyed those in the old cottage simply because they have an especially old-world feeling. Guests have an attractive little sitting room and breakfast room with little tables and chairs set in front of a dresser displaying decorative blue-and-white plates. Two modern kitchens are available for guests to prepare their picnics or suppers. Margaret and Ted supply guests with a map that outlines the vast array of places to visit in the area. *Directions:* From Stratford-upon-Avon take the A3400 signposted for Henley-in-Arden for 2½ miles. Turn left to Wilmcote and Pear Tree Cottage is in the center of the village.

PEAR TREE COTTAGE
Owners: Margaret & Ted Mander
Church Road
Wilmcote
Stratford-upon-Avon
Warwickshire CV37 9UX, England
Tel: (01789) 205889 Fax: (01789) 262862
7 en-suite rooms
From £20 per person
Closed Christmas
Children over 2

Nestled beside the baby River Isbourne on a quiet county lane just a few yards from the main street of the delightfully pretty Cotswold village of Winchcombe, Isbourne Manor House dates back to Elizabethan times with extensive Georgian additions. From the moment you enter you will be delighted by the attractive decor and warmth of hospitality offered by Rita and Graham. The elegant drawing room with its light-blue sofas and chairs is exclusively for guests' use. Breakfast is the only meal served round the antique refectory dining-room table, but the Smiths provide an extensive list of suggested eating places in the area. Splurge and request The Sudeley Room, well worth the few additional pounds to enjoy its elegant queen-sized four-poster bed swathed with peach-colored draperies. Langley is a most attractive double-bedded room decorated in shades of cream. Under the steeply sloping eaves of the Elizabethan portion of the house you find the snug quarters offered by Beesmore whose window serves as the door onto a large rooftop terrace (bathroom down the hall). Walk to nearby Sudeley Castle, more of a stately home than a traditional castle, then set out on Rita and Graham's day-long tour of Cotswold villages with Bourton-on-the-Water, Stow-on-the-Wold, Chipping Campden, and Broadway being popular destinations. *Directions:* Winchcombe is on the B4632 between Cheltenham and Broadway. Turn into Castle Street (in the center of the village) and Isbourne Manor House is on the left just before the little bridge.

ISBOURNE MANOR HOUSE   **NEW**
Owners: Rita & Graham Smith
Castle Street
Winchcombe
Gloucestershire GL54 6JA, England
Tel: (01242) 602281
3 rooms, 2 en suite
From £22 per person
Open all year
Children over 10
No-smoking house

Winchelsea is one of the earliest examples of town planning, having been rebuilt in 1277 after being devastated by the marauding French. The hilltop site is crowned by a church and surrounded by streets of enviable houses. Among the quiet byways are two pubs, a shop, a post office, and a tea shop (the Tea Tree). Set on a cliff overlooking the marshes, Cleveland House provides a serene contrast to the bustle of nearby Rye and a base for your explorations of southern Sussex and Kent. The Jempsons' 18th-century home is fronted by over an acre of manicured lawns, appealing flower borders, a walled vegetable garden, and a sheltered heated swimming pool (May to September). The house is furnished with antiques and from the flagstone hallway guests have their private staircase which leads to two pretty bedrooms. As you lie in bed in the front bedroom you have exquisite views through floor-length windows towards the distant sea. The bathroom is a few steps down the hall. The pretty twin-bedded room has a small shower room en suite. Both rooms have televisions and tea and coffee trays. Cliff, the gardener, is often on hand to discuss his vegetables and flowers and guests are encouraged to use the lovely swimming pool. Sitting rooms are reserved for family use. Breakfast is the only meal served. *Directions:* From Rye take the A259 to Winchelsea (2 miles). Go up the hill, through the arch, take the first left, and Cleveland House is the first home on the left.

CLEVELAND HOUSE
Owners: Sarah & Jonathan Jempson
Winchelsea
East Sussex TN36 4EE, England
Tel: (01797) 226256 Fax: (01797) 225080
2 rooms, 1 en suite
From £25 per person
Closed Christmas & New Year
Credit cards: MC, VS
Children welcome
No-smoking house

The Wykeham Arms is a very extraordinary Victorian pub: over 600 pictures decorate the walls, 1,000 tankards hang from beams, walls, and windows, and Winchester memorabilia abounds—many of the tables are old desks from nearby Winchester College. The menu, posted on the board in the bar, offers choices ranging from elaborate fare to tasty pub grub. Quieter tables can be reserved in the Bishop's Bar or the Watchmaker's Room with its pictures of an old-time watchmender. A family Bible sits atop a lectern outside the breakfast room. Up narrow stairways, the pretty bedrooms are not elaborate, but several have views across the chimney tops. Small refrigerators are stocked with very reasonably priced drinks. Because The Wykeham Arms is located in a pedestrian zone, all is peace and quiet (except on Friday morning when barrels of beer are rolled across the cobbles at 7:30 am). You can wander along the lovely old streets, stroll through the King's Gate and across the lawns to Winchester Cathedral with its seven chapels, medieval wall paintings, and royal tombs, and walk to everything in Winchester. *Directions:* Winchester is between junctions 9 and 10 on the M3. The Wykeham Arms is located near the cathedral. Graeme will send you a map which will enable you to navigate your car through the pedestrian zone to the pub's car park.

THE WYKEHAM ARMS
Owners: Anne & Graeme Jameson
75 Kingsgate Street
Winchester
Hampshire SO23 98T, England
Tel: (01962) 853834 Fax: (01962) 854411
7 en-suite rooms
From £37.50 per person
Open all year
Credit cards: all major
Children over 14

In the Lake District it seems that run-of-the-mill hotels and guesthouses are a dime a dozen, so I was thrilled when I found an exceptional one in The Archway Guest House in the center of Windermere village. Hosts Aurea and Tony Greenhalgh serve mouthwatering breakfasts which offer homemade yogurt sweetened with a dash of honey and topped with fruit puree, freshly squeezed juices, American pancakes with syrup, and apple griddle cakes with butter and syrup as well as a traditional farmhouse breakfast. The Greenhalghs pride themselves on serving homemade foods, using organic ingredients whenever possible. Dinners are fresh and delicious and are accompanied by a choice of six red and six white wines. All the rooms are decorated in keeping with a Victorian home, from country pine in the dining room to antique quilts gracing the beds. Up the narrow, steep stairs the bedrooms and bathrooms are small, even tiny, but are very well equipped. The Archway is located in the heart of the Lake District, an area known for its outstanding beauty. An information book in every bedroom lists walks in the area for which Tony supplies maps. More leisurely exercise can be obtained by strolling into town. *Directions:* Exit the M6 at junction 36 and take the A591 around Kendal towards Ambleside. Shortly after passing Windermere's train station, turn left on Elleray Road and right into College Road. The Archway is on the left.

THE ARCHWAY GUEST HOUSE
Owners: Aurea & Tony Greenhalgh
13 College Road
Windermere
Cumbria LA23 1BY, England
Tel: (015394) 45613
4 en-suite rooms
From £22 per person
Open all year
Credit cards: all major
Children over 10
No-smoking house

Hawksmoor Guest House appears no different from the many other guesthouses on these well traveled Lake District roads until one enters, sees, and appreciates the apple-pie-order of Barbara and Robert Tyson's home. The decor is not fancy or pretentious, for this is not an expensive country house hotel, but it is well maintained: Robert boasts, "If it's broken or damaged today, it will be fixed by tomorrow." The dining room is delightfully set with pink tablecloths covered with delicate lace and laid with silver service. Barbara is happy for guests to eat in or out, always willing to provide a traditional English three-course dinner. Guests have a small comfortable lounge at their disposal. The bedrooms are smallish but each is decorated with pretty flowered wallpaper with matching curtains and bedspreads, and all have en-suite bathrooms. Robert is an expert on the Lake District and even manages to suggest a sight or two to the hurried traveler who is dashing through this lovely part of England and using it as a one-night stop on the road between London and Edinburgh. He has found that these rushed travelers often return for a stay of several days. Windermere is in the heart of the busy southern Lake District, easily accessible from the M6. *Directions:* Windermere is just off the A591 Ambleside to Kendal road. Drive along New Road and look for Hawksmoor on the right just after the clock tower.

HAWKSMOOR GUEST HOUSE
Owners: Barbara & Robert Tyson
Lake Road
Windermere
Cumbria LA23 2EQ, England
Tel: (015394) 42110
10 en-suite rooms
From £24 per person
Closed December 1–25 & January 8–31
Credit cards: MC, VS
Children over 6

Just 5 miles from the Georgian splendors of Bath, Burghope Manor is the 13th-century home of Liz and John Denning. Much of the present house dates from Tudor times and Burghope has strong associations with Henry VIII's prelate Archbishop Cranmer. Liz is a vivacious person who loves meeting people from all walks of life and all over the world and enjoys sharing her lovely home with them. Guests are encouraged to make themselves at home in the large pink drawing room, though they often prefer the cozier confines of the morning room. Upstairs, the five spacious, lovely bedrooms are each accompanied by an en-suite bathroom with bath and shower. For dinner, guests stroll into Winsley, a typical old country village, to dine at the Seven Stars Pub or Nightingales Restaurant. If you are planning on staying a week or longer consider renting the Dower House, a luxurious three-bedroom, three-bathroom home sitting in the grounds of Burghope Manor. There are enough activities in Bath to occupy a week, though nearby Bradford on Avon should not be missed. *Directions:* From Bath take the A36 towards Warminster for 5 miles and turn left on the B3108 signposted Winsley and Bradford on Avon. Follow the road up into the village and, immediately after passing the 30 mph signs, turn left into a small lane to Burghope Manor.

BURGHOPE MANOR
Owners: Liz & John Denning
Winsley
Bradford on Avon
Wiltshire BA15 2LA, England
Tel: (01225) 723557 Fax: (01225) 723113
5 en-suite rooms
From £32.50 per person
Closed Christmas & New Year
Credit cards: all major
Children over 10

The Old Wharf's idyllic setting provides an entrancing first impression. A lane leading off the main highway wends its way down to a delightful small building hugging the edge of a tiny canal. Nearby, cows graze peacefully in meadows which stretch as far as the eye can see. The enclosed front patio is ablaze with a riot of color: a blowzy cottage garden of colorful flowers, beautifully manicured yet artfully exuberant. The side of the house that opens onto the meandering stream is laced with climbing pink roses. The spell of the initial impression remains unbroken when you go inside. Moira and David have taken an old warehouse and converted it into their home, incorporating an outstanding small bed and breakfast. The decor throughout is fresh and airy and extremely pretty. Moira has managed to cleverly combine lovely pastel fabrics with natural-wood-finish antiques to achieve a very pretty country look. Primrose has a small double-bedded bedroom and a snug sitting room with tall windows opening up to views of the river and fields. A Continental breakfast, the only meal served, is included in the tariff. Within easy reach are the towns of the Sussex coast, Petworth House, and Arundel Castle. *Directions:* From Billingshurst take the A272 towards Petworth, cross the canal and river, and The Old Wharf is 50 yards after the river on the left.

THE OLD WHARF
Owners: Moira & David Mitchell
Wisborough Green
Billingshurst
Sussex RH14 OJG, England
Tel: (01403) 784096 Fax: (01403) 784096
4 en suite rooms
From £22.50 per person
Closed Christmas & New Year
Credit cards: all major
Children over 12
No-smoking house

The attractive market town of Shrewsbury is a 20-minute drive from the quiet countryside hamlet of Woolstaston where you find Rectory Farm, built around 1620 in traditional Shropshire style with black timbers and white walls, sitting in a pretty garden with countryside views that stretch across the plains to Wales. John Davies was born here and now he and his wife Jeanette welcome bed and breakfast guests. Several cottagey little rooms have been combined to give guests a large sitting room either side of a massive stone fireplace. Narrow stairs wind round the fireplace to a delightful twin-bedded room set under the rafters. Up the equally narrow main staircase you find two additional bedrooms: an airy twin-bedded room large enough to accommodate a comfortable chintz-covered sofa and chair and a snug double-bedded room. Guests breakfast together in the dining room with its carved oak paneling and for dinner often go to The Botland Lass, just down the lane in Picklescott, or The Pound, a thatched pub in nearby Leebotwood. Perched on a hill in the midst of a great loop in the River Severn, Shrewsbury beckons to visitors—explore its winding lanes, the castle, its many museums, the market square, and its decorative black-and-white houses. For a glimpse of England's industrial heritage, visit the Ironbridge Gorge Museum at Telford with its fascinating displays, exhibits, and reconstructio s as well as the world's first iron bridge. *Directions:* From Shrewsbury take the A49 (towards Leominster) to Leebotwood where you turn right for Woolstaston. Rectory Farm is on your right in the center of the village.

RECTORY FARM   **NEW**
Owners: Jeanette & John Davies
Woolstaston, Church Stretton
Shropshire SY6 6NN, England
Tel: (01694) 751306
3 en-suite rooms
From £20 per person
Open all year
Children over 12

18 St. Paul's Square is one of several large Victorian terrace homes which border a grassy square down one of York's quiet side streets. From the outside, it looks just like many other houses in this up-and-coming neighborhood, but inside it is delightfully different, showcasing colorful country-Victorian decor by Ann and Mike Beaufoy. A sunny yellow hallway rises from the entry, setting the cheerful mood felt throughout the house. In the sitting room sage-green leafy wallpaper serves as a backdrop for an old country dresser displaying blue-and-white willow dishes and an old gray-marble fireplace looking much as it must have done in Victorian times. The bedrooms are spacious and airy. I particularly admired the double room with warm-pine furniture and a brass-and-iron bedstead covered with a patchwork bedspread. It is a ten-minute walk from St. Paul's Square to the walls which surround the historic city center. For sightseeing, after you have exhausted the many possibilities in York, there are excursions to the North York Moors and the Dales and tours of stately homes (Castle Howard is a must) and ecclesiastical ruins (Rievaulx and Fountains Abbey). *Directions:* Leave the A64, York ring road, at the A1036 in the direction of York city center. Pass the racecourse and as the walls of York come into view, turn left on Holgate Road (A59 Harrogate). After crossing the railway tracks, look for a right turn to St. Paul's Square.

18 ST. PAUL'S SQUARE
Owners: Ann & Mike Beaufoy
18 St. Paul's Square
York YO2 4BD, England
Tel: (01904) 629884
3 rooms, 2 en suite
From £30 per person
Closed Christmas
Children welcome
Wolsey Lodge

Just a few yards from York's city walls, South Parade is a private, cobbled street adjacent to a very busy main road. Inside Number 4 is a world of quiet repose, where you are invited to partake of tea and hot buttered scones in the elegant drawing room. Bedrooms are all furnished to the highest standards: bathrooms are sparkling and have powerful showers, brass fittings, and are well equipped with many extras. All the rooms are decorated in soft pastels, one in soft blue-grays, another in shades of peach with matching bedspreads and drapes coordinating with the wall covering. On the top floor, a larger suite with a sitting area and writing desk gives guests lots of room for relaxation should they prefer the privacy of their room to the drawing room. Meals are taken in the below-stairs room that was once the kitchen—with advance notice Anne is happy to provide a three-course candlelit supper. Anne and Robin are mines of information on York and the surrounding countryside and they really put themselves out to steer visitors in the right direction. Guests often enjoy a bus tour of the Dales and Moors. *Directions:* Leave the A64 (which forms the southern part of the York Outer Ring Road) at the A1036, in the direction of York city center, following signs for the racecourse. Pass the racecourse, and as you see the Odeon Cinema on the left, turn right into a narrow street (next to a car showroom) which is South Parade.

4 SOUTH PARADE
Owners: Anne & Robin McClure
4 South Parade
York YO2 2BA, England
Tel & fax: (01904) 628229
3 en-suite rooms
From £35 per person
Closed Christmas
Children not accepted
No-smoking house

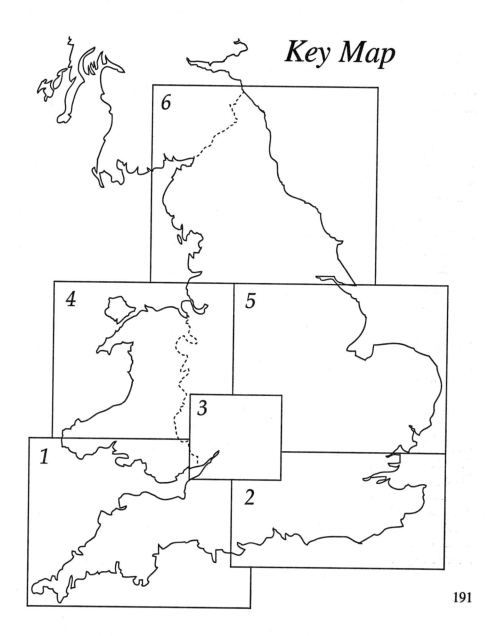

Key Map

6

4

5

3

1

2

191

Map 1

WALES

CHELTENHAM

Willersey
Broadway
Rendcomb
Oaksey
Ashton Keynes
Dursley
Grittleton
Nettleton
Calne
M4
Bathford
BATH
Bradford on Avon
Winsley
Norton St. Philip
Salisbury
M50
M5

St. Briavels

M4

BRISTOL CHANNEL

BRISTOL

Wells
Glastonbury
Stoke St. Gregory
Somerton
Marnhull

Porlock
Dunster
Stogumber
Holford
Huish Champflower
Curry Rivel
Beercrocombe
East Coker

Parkham
Brithem Bottom
Honiton
Frampton
Affpuddle

- Places to Stay
○ Orientation / Sightseeing
✈ Airport

a	b
c	d

Quadrants

North Bovey
EXETER
Dorchester

Tintagel
Crackington Haven
Drewsteignton
Manaton
Chudleigh
Haytor Vale
Shaldon
Teignmouth
ENGLISH CHANNEL
Bucknowle

A39
A30
A30
A38

Lanhydrock
Polperro
Dartington
Dartmouth

St Blazey

PLYMOUTH
Noss Mayo

Penzance
Penryn
Constantine
Golsithney
Lizard

A30

Map 2

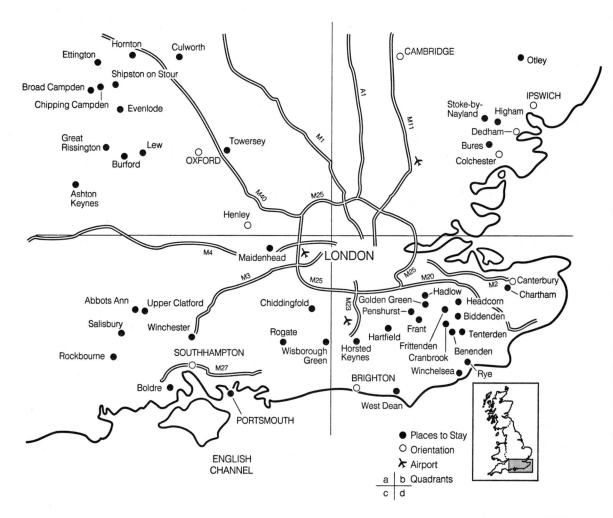

Hornton
Culworth
Ettington
Shipston on Stour
Broad Campden
Chipping Campden
Evenlode
Great Rissington
Lew
Towersey
OXFORD
Burford
Ashton Keynes
Henley
M40
M25
M1

CAMBRIDGE
Otley
A1
M11
Stoke-by-Nayland
Higham
IPSWICH
Dedham—
Bures
Colchester

M4
Maidenhead
LONDON
M3
M25
M25
M20
M2
Canterbury
Chartham
Golden Green
Hadlow
Headcorn
Penshurst
Biddenden
Abbots Ann
Upper Clatford
Chiddingfold
M23
Frant
Salisbury
Winchester
Rogate
Hartfield
Tenterden
Frittenden
Rockbourne
Wisborough Green
Horsted Keynes
Cranbrook
Benenden
SOUTHHAMPTON
Winchelsea
Rye
M27
BRIGHTON
Boldre
West Dean
PORTSMOUTH

ENGLISH CHANNEL

● Places to Stay
O Orientation
✈ Airport

| a | b | Quadrants |
| c | d | |

193

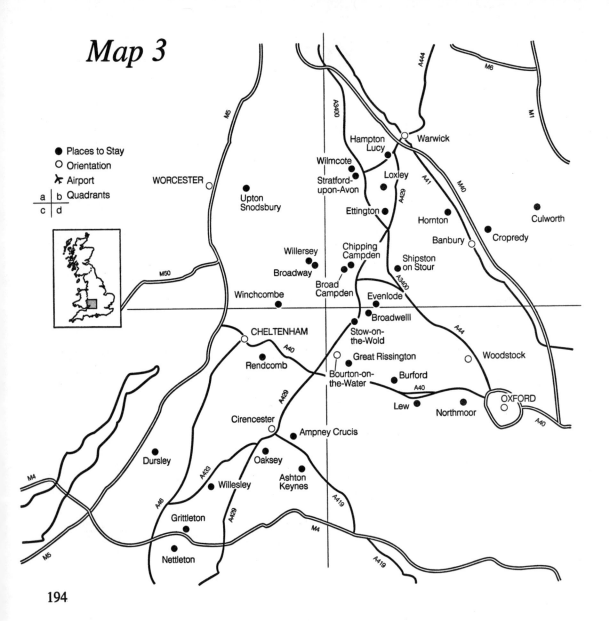

Map 3

● Places to Stay
○ Orientation
✈ Airport

| a | b | Quadrants |
| c | d | |

WORCESTER

Upton Snodsbury

M5

M50

Hampton Lucy
Warwick
Wilmcote
Loxley
Stratford-upon-Avon
Ettington
Hornton
Culworth
Banbury
Cropredy
Willersey
Chipping Campden
Shipston on Stour
Broadway
Broad Campden
Winchcombe
Evenlode
Broadwelll
Stow-on-the-Wold
CHELTENHAM
Rendcomb
Great Rissington
Woodstock
Bourton-on-the-Water
Burford
Lew
Northmoor
OXFORD
Cirencester
Ampney Crucis
Dursley
Oaksey
Ashton Keynes
Willesley
Grittleton
Nettleton

A444
M6
M1
A3400
A41
M40
A429
A3400
A44
A40
A429
A433
A46
A429
A419
M4
A419
A40
M4
M5

194

Map 4

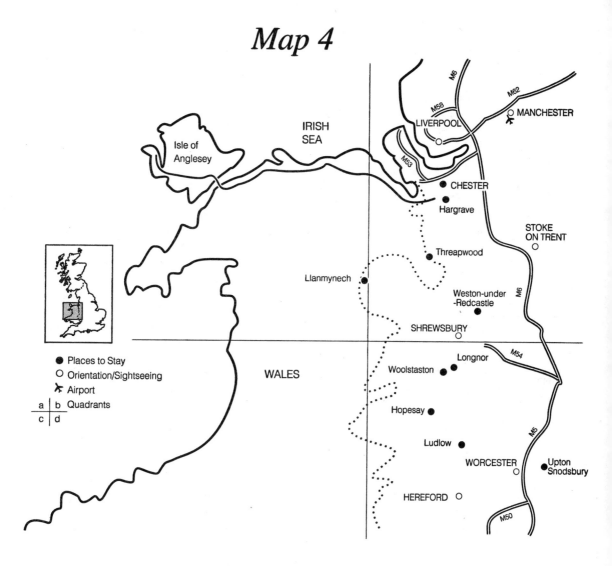

IRISH
SEA

Isle of
Anglesey

MANCHESTER

LIVERPOOL

M6

M62

M58

M53

CHESTER

Hargrave

STOKE
ON TRENT

Threapwood

Llanmynech

Weston-under
-Redcastle

M6

SHREWSBURY

WALES

Longnor

M54

Woolstaston

Hopesay

Ludlow

M5

WORCESTER

Upton
Snodsbury

HEREFORD

M50

● Places to Stay
○ Orientation/Sightseeing
✈ Airport

a	b
c	d

Quadrants

195

Map 5

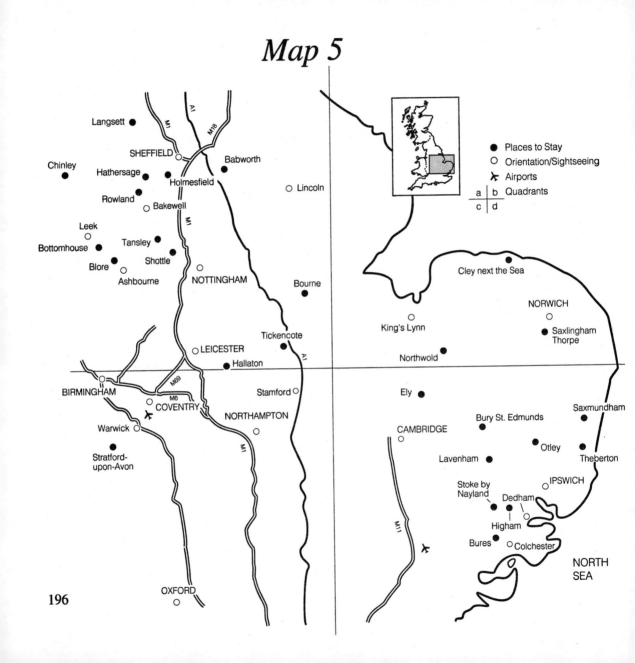

Langsett ●

SHEFFIELD

Chinley ●

Hathersage ●

Rowland ●

Holmesfield ●

Bakewell ○

Babworth ●

○ Lincoln

Leek ○

Bottomhouse ●

Tansley ●

Blore ●

Shottle ●

Ashbourne ○

NOTTINGHAM ○

Bourne ●

Cley next the Sea ●

NORWICH ●

King's Lynn ○

Saxlingham Thorpe ●

Tickencote ●

LEICESTER ○

Hallaton ●

Northwold ●

Stamford ○

Ely ●

BIRMINGHAM ○

COVENTRY ○

NORTHAMPTON ○

Warwick ○

Stratford-upon-Avon ●

CAMBRIDGE ○

Bury St. Edmunds ●

Saxmundham ●

Otley ●

Theberton ●

Lavenham ●

Stoke by Nayland ●

Dedham ●

IPSWICH ○

Higham ●

Bures ●

Colchester ○

NORTH SEA

OXFORD ○

Legend

● Places to Stay
○ Orientation/Sightseeing
✈ Airports

a	b
c	d

Quadrants

196

Map 6

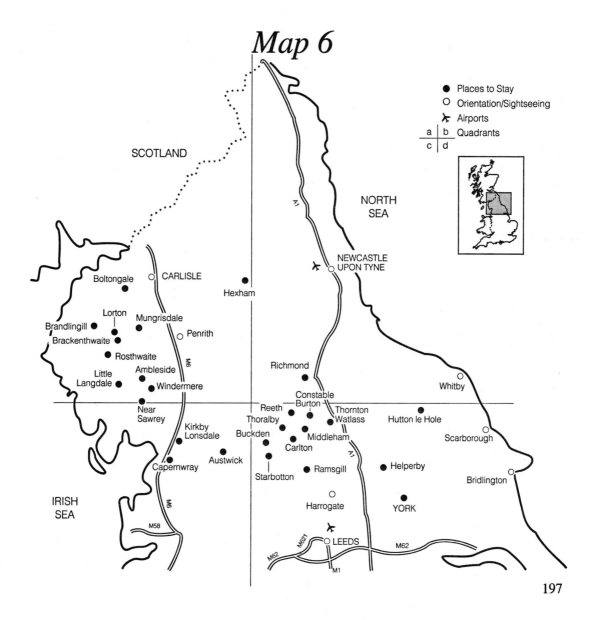

SCOTLAND

NORTH
SEA

● Places to Stay
○ Orientation/Sightseeing
✈ Airports
a | b   Quadrants
c | d

○ CARLISLE

Boltongale ●

● Hexham

Lorton ●
Brandlingill ●   ● Mungrisdale
Brackenthwaite ●
                  ○ Penrith
● Rosthwaite

Little ● Ambleside
Langdale ● ● Windermere

Near
Sawrey

Kirkby
Lonsdale
● Buckden
● Capernwray   ● Austwick

● Starbotton

IRISH
SEA

A1

✈ NEWCASTLE
   UPON TYNE ○

M6

● Richmond

Constable
Burton
● Reeth
Thoralby
              ● Thornton
              Watlass   ● Hutton le Hole
● Carlton
Middleham

● Ramsgill   ● Helperby

○ Harrogate

✈ LEEDS ○

M58
M62   M621   M62
              M1

A1

○ Whitby

○ Scarborough

● Bridlington

● YORK

197

Places That Welcome Children

(no age limit)

Ashton Keynes, Cove House
Babworth, The Barns
Bath, Haydon House
Bath, Holly Lodge
Boldre, Boldre Hill
Bottomhouse, Pethills Bank Cottage
Bourne, Bourne Eau House
Bucknowle, Bucknowle House
Broad Campden, The Malt House
Broadway, Milestone House
Buckden, The Buck Inn
Burford, The Lamb Inn
Carlton, Foresters Arms
Chiddingfold, Greenaway
Constable Burton, Sun Hill
Constantine, Treviades Barton
Cropredy, The Old Manor
Dartmouth, Ford House
Dursley–Stinchcombe, Drakestone House
East Coker–Holywell, Holywell House
Frant, The Old Parsonage
Goldsithney, Ennys Farm
Great Rissington, The Lamb Inn
Hargrave, Greenlooms Cottage
Haytor Vale, The Rock Inn
Helperby, Brafferton Hall
Hexham, East Peterel Field Farm
Higham, The Old Vicarage
Holford, Quantock House
Hornton, The Manor House

Hutton le Hole, Hammer and Hand
Lavenham, The Great House
Little Langdale, Three Shires Inn
Llanmynech, Vyrnwy Bank
Loxley, Loxley Farm
Manaton, Barracott
Marnhull, Old Lamb House
Middleham, Waterford House
Mungrisdale, The Mill Hotel
Nettleton, Fosse Farmhouse
Norton St. Philip, The Plaine Guest House
Ramsgill, The Yorke Arms
Reeth, The Burgoyne Hotel
Rowland, Holly Cottage
Rye, Jeake's House
Saxmundham–Hinton, High Poplars
Shipston on Stour, Longdon Manor
Shottle, Dannah Farm
Somerton, The Lynch Country House
St. Briavels, Cinderhill House
Starbotton, Hilltop Country Guest House
Tansley, Lane End House
Upper Clatford, Malt Cottage
Wells, Beryl
Winchelsea, Cleveland House
York, 18 St. Paul's Square

No-Smoking Houses

Ampney Crucis, Waterton Garden Cottage
Bath, Haydon House
Bath, Holly Lodge
Bath, Somerset House
Biddenden, River Hall Coach House
Boltongate, The Old Rectory
Brackenthwaite, Pickett Howe
Brandlingill, Low Hall
Brithem Bottom, Lower Beers
Broad Campden, Orchard Hill House
Bury St. Edmunds, Twelve Angel Hill
Cropredy, The Old Manor
Dunster, Dollons House
Dursley–Stinchcombe, Drakestone House
Ettington, Ettington Manor
Frittenden, Maplehurst Mill
Golden Green, Goldhill Mill
Hadlow, Leavers Oast
Hartfield, Bolebroke Mill
Headcorn, Vine Farm
Holford, Quantock House
Horsted Keynes, Rixons
Langsett, Alderman's Head Manor
Lanhydrock, Treffry Farmhouse
Lizard, Landewednack House
Lorton, New House Farm
Ludlow, Number Eleven
Maidenhead, Beehive Manor
Marnhull, Old Lamb House
Northmoor, Rectory Farm
Norton St. Philip, The Plaine Guest House
Noss Mayo–Bridgend, Rowan Cottage

Oaksey, Oaksey Court
Oxford, Cotswold House
Parkham, The Old Rectory
Penryn, Clare House
Penshurst, Swale Cottage
Polperro–Pelynt, Trenderway Farm
Porlock, Bales Mead
Rogate, Mizzards Farm
Rosthwaite, Hazel Bank
Rye, Green Hedges
Salisbury, Stratford Lodge
Shipston on Stour, Longdon Manor
St. Blazey, Nanscawen House
Stogumber, Curdon Mill
Tansley, Lane End House
Tenterden, Brattle House
Threapwood, Broughton House
Towersey, Upper Green Farm
West Dean, The Old Parsonage
Weston-under-Redcastle, The Citadel
Willersey, The Old Rectory
Winchcombe, Isbourne Manor House
Winchelsea, Cleveland House
Windermere, The Archway Guest House
Wisborough Green, The Old Wharf
York, 4 South Parade

Members of Wolsey Lodges

Ashton Keynes, Cove House
Blore, The Old Rectory
Boldre, Boldre Hill
Boltongate, The Old Rectory
Bourne, Bourne Eau House
Bradford on Avon, Priory Steps
Brithem Bottom, Lower Beers
Calne, Chilvester Hill House
Capernwray, New Capernwray Farm
Chinley, Ashen Clough
Chudleigh, Oakfield
Cranbrook, The Old Cloth Hall
Dursley–Stinchcombe, Drakestone House
Ettington, Ettington Manor
Frittenden, Maplehurst Mill
Hallaton, The Old Rectory
Helperby, Brafferton Hall

Higham, The Old Vicarage
Honiton, Woodhayes
Horsted Keynes, Rixons
Huish Champflower, Jews Farm House
Longnor, Moat House
Ludlow, The Lodge
Noss Mayo–Bridgend, Rowan Cottage
Oaksey, Oaksey Court
Saxmundham–Hinton, High Poplars
Teignmouth, Thomas Luny House
Tenterden, Brattle House
Thoralby, Littleburn
Tickencote, Tickencote Hall
Upton Snodsbury, Upton House
Wells, Beryl
Weston-under-Redcastle, The Citadel
York, 18 St. Paul's Square

Index

A

Abbotts Ann
  Abbotts Law, 16
Affpuddle
  The Old Vicarage, 17
Alderman's Head Manor, Langsett, 104, 199
Alveston Cottage, Stratford-upon-Avon, 161
Ambleside
  Grey Friar Lodge, 18
Ampney Crucis
  Waterton Garden Cottage, 19, 199
Angel Inn, The, Stoke by Nayland, 158
Archway Guest House, The, Windermere, 184, 199
Ashen Clough, Chinley, 55, 200
Ashton Keynes
  Cove House, 20, 198, 200
Austwick
  Wood View, 21

B

Babworth
  The Barns, 22, 198
Bales Mead, Porlock, 134
Barns, The, Babworth, 22, 198
Barracott, Manaton, 115, 198

Bath
  Haydon House, 23, 198, 199
  Holly Lodge, 24, 198, 199
  Somerset House, 25, 199
Bathford
  The Orchard, 26
Bed and Breakfast Travel (Introduction), 2
  Animals, 2
  Arrival and Departure, 2
  Bathrooms, 2
  Bedrooms, 3
  Children, 3
  Christmas, 3
  Credit Cards, 4
  Directions, 4
  Electricity, 4
  Maps, 5
  Meals, 5
  Rates, 6
  Reservations, 6
  Sightseeing, 8
  Smoking, 8
  Socializing, 9
  Wolsey Lodges, 9
Beehive Manor, Maidenhead, 114, 199

C

D

Greenlooms Cottage, Hargrave, 86, 198
Grey Friar Lodge, Ambleside, 18
Grittleton
    Church House, 82

H

Hadlow
    Leavers Oast, 83, 199
Hallaton
    The Old Rectory, 84, 200
Hammer & Hand Guest House, Hutton le Hole, 100, 198
Hampton Lucy
    Sandbarn Farm, 85
Hancocks Farmhouse, Cranbrook, 62
Hargrave
    Greenlooms Cottage, 86, 198
Hartfield
    Bolebroke Mill, 87, 199
Hathersage
    Carr Head Farm, 88
Hawksmoor Guest House, Windermere, 185
Haydon House, Bath, 23, 198, 199
Haytor Vale
    The Rock Inn, 89, 198
Hazel Bank, Rosthwaite, 141, 199
Headcorn
    Vine Farm, 90, 199

Helperby
    Brafferton Hall, 91, 198, 200
Hexham
    East Peterel Field Farm, 92, 198
High Green House, Thoralby, 166
High Poplars, Saxmundham–Hinton, 149, 198, 200
Higham
    The Old Vicarage, 93, 198, 200
Hillards, Curry Rivel, 66
Hilltop Country Guest House, Starbotton, 156, 198
Hipping Hall, Kirkby Lonsdale, 103
Holford
    Quantock House, 94, 198, 199
Holly Cottage, Rowland, 142, 198
Holly Lodge, Bath, 24, 198, 199
Holmesfield
    Horsleygate Hall, 95
Holywell House, East Coker, 72, 198
Honiton
    Woodhayes, 96, 200
Hornton
    The Manor House, 97, 198
Horsleygate Hall, Holmesfield, 95
Horsted Keynes
    Rixons, 98, 199, 200
Huish Champflower
    Jews Farm House, 99, 200

M

Maidenhead
Beehive Manor, 114, 199
Malt Cottage, Upper Clatford, 173, 198
Malt House, The, Broad Campden, 41, 198
Manaton
Barracott, 115, 198
Manor House, The, Hornton, 97, 198
Maplehurst Mill, Frittenden, 78, 199, 200
Marnhull
Old Lamb House, 116, 198, 199
Middleham
Waterford House, 117, 198
Milestone House, Broadway, 43, 198
Mill Hotel, The, Mungrisdale, 118, 198
Mizzards Farm, Rogate, 140, 199
Moat House, Longnor, 110, 200
Mungrisdale
The Mill Hotel, 118, 198

N

Nanscawen House, St. Blazey, 154, 199
Near Sawrey
Ees Wyke Country House Hotel, 119
Nettleton
Fosse Farmhouse, 120, 198

New Capernwray Farm, Capernwray, 51, 200
New House Farm, Lorton, 102, 199
North Bovey
Gate House, 121
Northmoor
Rectory Farm, 122, 199
Northwold
The Grange, 123
Norton St. Philip
The Plaine Guest House, 124, 198, 199
Noss Mayo–Bridgend
Rowan Cottage, 125, 199, 200
Number Eleven, Ludlow, 112, 199

O

Oakfield, Chudleigh, 57, 200
Oaksey
Oaksey Court, 126, 199, 200
Old Cloth Hall, The, Cranbrook, 63, 200
Old Lamb House, Marnhull, 116, 198, 199
Old Manor, The, Cropredy, 64, 198, 199
Old Parsonage, The, Frant, 77, 198
Old Parsonage, The, West Dean, 176, 199
Old Rectory, The, Blore, 31, 200
Old Rectory, The, Boltongate, 33, 199, 200
Old Rectory, The, Hallaton, 84, 200
Old Rectory, The, Parkham, 129, 199

T

Index

SEAL COVE INN—LOCATED IN THE SAN FRANCISCO AREA

Karen Brown Herbert (best known as author of the Karen Brown's guides) and her husband, Rick, have put 19 years of experience into reality and opened their own superb hideaway, Seal Cove Inn. Spectacularly set amongst wild flowers and bordered by towering cypress trees, Seal Cove Inn looks out to the ocean over acres of county park: an oasis where you can enjoy secluded beaches, explore tidepools, watch frolicking seals, and follow the tree-lined path that traces the windswept ocean bluffs. Country antiques, original watercolors, flower-laden cradles, rich fabrics, and the gentle ticking of grandfather clocks create the perfect ambiance for a foggy day in front of the crackling log fire. Each bedroom is its own haven with a cozy sitting area before a wood-burning fireplace and doors opening onto a private balcony or patio with views to the distant ocean. Moss Beach is a 35-minute drive south of San Francisco, 6 miles north of the picturesque town of Half Moon Bay, and a few minutes from Princeton harbor with its colorful fishing boats and restaurants. Seal Cove Inn makes a perfect base for whale-watching, salmon-fishing excursions, day trips to San Francisco, exploring the coast, or, best of all, just a romantic interlude by the sea, time to relax and be pampered. Karen and Rick look forward to the pleasure of welcoming you to their hideaway by the sea.

Seal Cove Inn, 221 Cypress Avenue, Moss Beach, California 94038, USA
Telephone: (415) 728-7325   Fax: (415) 728-4116

We Love to Hear from Karen Brown's Readers

ACCOLADES: We'd love to hear which accommodations you have especially enjoyed—even the shortest of notes is greatly appreciated. It is reassuring to know that places we recommend meet with your approval.

COMPLAINTS: Please let us know when a place we recommend fails to live up to the standards you have come to expect from Karen Brown. Constructive criticism is greatly appreciated. We sometimes make a mistake, places change, or go downhill. Your letters influence us to re-evaluate a listing.

RECOMMENDATIONS: If you have a favorite hideaway that you would like to recommend, please write to us. Give us a feel for the place, if possible send us a brochure and photographs (which we regret we cannot return). Convince us that on our next research trip, your discovery deserves a visit. All accommodations included in our guides are ones we have seen and enjoyed. Many of our finest selections are those that readers have discovered—wonderful places we would never have found on our own.

Please send information to:

KAREN BROWN'S GUIDES
Post Office Box 70
San Mateo, California 94401, USA
Telephone: (415) 342-9117   Fax: (415) 342-9153

Be a Karen Brown's Preferred Reader

If you would like to be the first to know when new editions of Karen Brown's Guides go to press, and also to be included in any special promotions, simply send us your name and address. We encourage you to buy new editions and throw away the old ones so that you don't miss a wealth of wonderful new discoveries or run the risk of staying in places that no longer meet our standards. We cover the miles searching for special places so that you don't have to spend your valuable vacation time doing so.

Name _____

Street _____

Town _____ State _____ Zip _____

Telephone: _____ Fax: _____

Please send information to:

KAREN BROWN'S GUIDES
Post Office Box 70
San Mateo, California 94401, USA
Telephone: (415) 342-9117   Fax: (415) 342-9153

JUNE BROWN's love of travel was inspired by the *National Geographic* magazines she read as a girl in her dentist's office—to date she has visited over 40 countries. June hails from Sheffield, England and lived in Zambia and Canada before moving to northern California where she lives in San Mateo with her husband, Tony, and their children, Simon and Clare.

BARBARA TAPP, the talented artist who produces all of the hotel sketches and delightful illustrations in this guide, was raised in Australia where she studied in Sydney at the School of Interior Design. Although Barbara continues with freelance projects, she devotes much of her time to illustrating the Karen Brown guides. Barbara lives in Kensington, California, with her husband, Richard, their two sons, Jonothan and Alexander, and daughter, Georgia.

JANN POLLARD, the artist responsible for the beautiful painting on the cover of this guide, has studied art since childhood, and is well-known for her outstanding impressionistic-style watercolors which she has exhibited in numerous juried shows, winning many awards. Jann travels frequently to Europe (using Karen Brown's guides) where she loves to paint historic buildings. Jann lives in Burlingame, California, with her husband, Gene.

NOTES

USA Order Form

Please ask in your local bookstore for KAREN BROWN'S GUIDES. If the books you want are unavailable, you may order directly from the publisher.

Austria: Charming Inns & Itineraries $16.95

California: Charming Inns & Itineraries $16.95

England: Charming Bed & Breakfasts $15.95

England, Wales & Scotland: Charming Hotels & Itineraries $16.95

French Country Bed & Breakfasts $15.95

France: Charming Inns & Itineraries $16.95

Germany: Charming Inns & Itineraries $16.95

Ireland: Charming Inns & Itineraries $16.95

Italy: Charming Bed & Breakfasts $15.95

Italy: Charming Inns & Itineraries $16.95

Spain: Charming Inns & Itineraries $16.95

Swiss Country Inns & Itineraries $16.95

Name _____ Street _____

Town _____ State _____ Zip _____ Tel. _____

Credit Card (MasterCard or Visa) _____ Exp. _____

Add $4 for the first book and 50 cents for each additional book for postage & packing. California residents add 8.25% sales tax. Order form **only** for shipments within the USA. Indicate number of copies of each title; send form with check or credit card information to:

KAREN BROWN'S GUIDES
Post Office Box 70, San Mateo, California, 94401
Telephone: (415) 342-9117   Fax: (415) 342-9153